S0-BSJ-054

FOUR FREEDOMS AND GOD

FOUR FREEDOMS
AND GOD

Edwin McNeill Poteat

Publishers

HARPER & BROTHERS

NEW YORK *and* LONDON

FOUR FREEDOMS AND GOD

This book is complete and unabridged
in contents, and is manufactured in strict
conformity with Government regulations
for saving paper.

To
THE FELLOWSHIP
OF
THE EUCLID AVENUE BAPTIST CHURCH
OF CLEVELAND, OHIO
THIS BOOK IS
AFFECTIONATELY INSCRIBED

ACKNOWLEDGMENTS

Grateful acknowledgment is made to the following publishers for their generous permission to use materials issued under their copyrights:

Walter Lippmann and the New York Herald-Tribune for the quotations from Mr. Lippmann's column, *Today and Tomorrow,* of December 2, 1942 and December 24, 1942; Dorothy Thompson and the Bell Syndicate for the quotation from Miss Thompson's column, *On the Record,* of December 23, 1942; the Yale University Press for the quotation from *Shadow Verses,* by Gamaliel Bradford; the Macmillan Company for the quotation from *Poems,* by John Masefield; the E. P. Dutton & Co., Inc. for the quotation from *Songs and Laughter,* by Arthur Guiterman; Charles Scribner's Sons for the quotation from *The Last Puritan,* by George Santayana; the New York World-Telegram for the quotations from Westbrook Pegler's column, *Fair Enough,* of December 30, 1942.

I wish also to thank Miss Anita Fahrenthold for her patient and good natured labor at the typewriter, preparing the manuscript.

E. M. P.

Bay Village, Ohio,
January 12, 1943

CONTENTS

Then the chief captain came, and said unto him, Tell me, art thou a Roman? He said, Yes.

And the chief captain answered, With a great sum obtained I this freedom. And Paul said, But I was born free.

Then straightway they departed from him which should have tortured him, and the chief captain also was afraid, after he knew that he was a Roman, and because he had bound him.

ACTS 22: 27-29

FOUR FREEDOMS AND GOD

One letter killeth; the spirit giveth life.
                                II Cor. 3:6

Here the free spirit of mankind, at length
Throws its last fetters off; and who shall place
A limit to the giant's unchained strength
Or curb his swiftness in the forward race?
                WILLIAM CULLEN BRYANT, *The Ages*

INTRODUCTION

"Freedom must be discovered and revealed in the experience of the spiritual life, for it is impossible to demonstrate it or deduce it from the nature of things."[1]

When on January 6, 1942, the President of the United States of America addressed the Congress on the state of the nation, he said, among other things: "Our objectives are clear . . . establishing and securing freedom of speech, freedom of religion, freedom from want and freedom from fear everywhere in the world."[2] This, by the easy test of quotability, is the most memorable sentence in his address. It gave instantaneous currency to what is now known as the Four Freedoms. Indeed it had the perhaps unexpected result of dimming out the eight principles of the much more pretentious

[1] Nikolai Berdyaev: *Freedom and the Spirit.* New York: Charles Scribner's Sons, 1935, page 117.

[2] From the full text of the President's message as printed in *Current History*, March, 1942.

1

Atlantic Charter which had been set forth many months earlier. It is not improbable that some of the lack of enthusiasm for the charter is to be explained partially by the annunciation of the freedoms, since the latter, by the single fact of their brevity conveyed the mistaken impression of being twice as easy to comprehend and achieve as the former which was twice as long.

So it has come about that the Four Freedoms have become *the* slogan on which the Allied Nations' will-to-win the war has been riding for more than twelve months. First in its vagueness, second in its brevity and third in the exemption it grants those who are disinclined to any very sustained reflection on war aims, it meets the standard requirements for the perfect slogan. That the third requirement is being generally met is indicated by the casual use of the phrase in radio programs and its careless use in public speeches. There is danger in the assumption of some of its users, that having quoted the President, they have practically created a new world.

Some there are who are trying in this connection to prevent the slow death that is the fate of most ideas that have frozen into slogans. These persons do not have much time on the radio, for, unfortunately the radio has not much time for them. I have encountered only one editorial discussion of the Freedoms. It was in a monthly trade journal. The official commentary by the O.W.I.

is a streamlined publicity release. But even such tries at salvage are approached mostly from the political angle as if the Freedoms could be understood primarily in political terms or achieved by political expedients.

Whether or not the President is aware of the fact, it is nevertheless true that he has set forth as the aims of the present armed struggle the strategy for a spiritual Armageddon; for the spiritual security and permanence of the new world will be won only by conclusive victories in the four fields mentioned. And the conclusive character of such victory will be manifest only in the realm of the human spirit. Political freedom of speech, or religion, from want and from fear will be at best inconclusive, and what we are determined to achieve this time is the sort of conquest that will stay put.

There are many, of course, who will shrug impatiently at such emphasis on the idea of spirit, and others who will insist honestly that the word communicates nothing to them. Their only approach to an understanding therefore will be political. As such their efforts should and shall be supported. Perhaps, however, they are not as obtuse concerning the spirit as they have been saying they were for the past twenty-five years. The word itself, discarded for a generation by careful and sensitive writers has enjoyed a return to respectability even if it still lacks the precision once claimed for it. At least it is something that responsible men are now speaking of spiritual things without stammering, and many writers whose interests would perhaps be described as dominantly secular, can now indite the weird word without blotting the page. Mr. Lippmann in his syndicated essay of December 2, 1942, sounded an emphasis that many other publicists are now making when he wrote:

No one is a genuine realist who forgets or ignores the will of man and least of all in the awful ordeal of war when men face the ultimate issues of life and death. The realism of Petain ended the other day in the tragic suicide of the demoralized and cornered navy of France. Let us not be deceived by the little realists into thinking anything durable can be built upon the foundations of that disaster, or that an expedient is anything more than an expedient to be administered lucidly, generously, but firmly and with confident self respect.[3]

This sets forth the significance of Toulon in essentially spiritual terms, and it would interest, though not so certainly gratify such men to know that their ideas when pressed to their limit, ultimately converge upon a sentence from one of the most learned of modern theologians.[4] From the same book quoted at the head of this chapter the following is lifted:

Spirit is the sphere in which the divine and human are united and it includes all man's aspirations after God and

[3] Copyright, 1942, New York *Tribune* Inc.

[4] Herbert Agar, Lewis Mumford, and Archibald MacLeish are also representative of this new mood.

the whole spiritual culture of man . . . all the intellectual, moral, and artistic life of humanity, all fellowship in love.[5]

By no means is it stated that these men would use all those words with the exact connotation the erudite Russian gives them; but they would certainly agree, as a minimum, that aspiration and culture are spiritual experiences and are as little amenable to the tricks and maulings of modern politics as are the tides and the weather. To use Lippmann's phrase again: an expedient is only an expedient. To deal adequately with life then, one must get beneath expedient to spirit.

As a matter of fact, we are beginning to learn that freedom is a spiritual experience, and for this elemental reason cannot be politically apprehended or organized. Insofar as this is true it lends support to what philosophy calls Spiritual Realism which is the theory that only the truly good will is free, and that events happen because of the rational, moral, and aesthetic activities of the finite mind, or by the animating and energizing principle of the Cosmos. There are, it says, two foci of progress: one is self-realization through experiencing the intangibles in the scale of human values—integrity, love, courage, sacrifice, freedom, etc. Ted Robinson, the sage who calls himself the Philosopher of Folly and daily conducts in the Cleveland *Plain Dealer* the wisest of columns, makes a similar list in his essay of January

[5] *Op. cit.* page 47.

2, 1943; "tolerance, justice, integrity, morality, art, literature, the expanding of knowledge and spirituality —the things that really characterize civilization." The second focus is the realization of God as the most important fact of all experience since He is ultimately determinative of everything. These aims are to be sought, as Ravaison put it, by an artless discipline: "To simplify one's self." If this seems rather too streamlined for our pedestrian minds, it is however, nothing less than what Philip Wylie, distinguished writer of light fiction, has proposed as the thesis of his timely and mordant book[6] which is a secularist's discussion of the proposition: "Resolved that Americans have lost their moral sensibilities by living too objectively and with too little subjective awareness." Mr. Wylie may be surprised to learn that his reputation as a short story writer is being dimmed by his rising repute as a philosopher of the school of the Spiritual Realists.

If then freedom of the spirit is absent from political freedom, political freedom becomes spiritual tyranny, and that means that the thing—whatever it is called— that politics has won, cannot survive if human spirits are alive to their condition. In other words the President's Four Freedoms cannot be won except they are spiritually won; nor can they be sustained except they

[6] *Generation of Vipers*. New York: Farrar & Rinehart, Inc., 1942.

be spiritually sustained. This is what Berdyaev means in the first quotation he supplied us.

Having said this, it is but a step to the claim that the Four Freedoms must become the primary concern of those who share the great Judeo-Christian cultural tradition, a tradition that is basically religious. There is very grave danger that the Four Freedoms, converted into a slogan and used for political or propaganda purposes primarily may become, after the military phase of the current world revolution is spent, the same sort of joke that "the war to end war" and "the war to make the world safe for democracy" became after World War I. Those were warm and inspiriting words to millions while that war was being fought; after it was over—if it ever was—those same words evoked the scorn of the cynic and the disillusioned. It is not reassuring to those who hold our religious cultural tradition in respect and devotion to contemplate the possibility of the ribald and the sneering in a new postwar atmosphere, taking out their spite on freedom of speech, freedom of religion, freedom from want and freedom from fear because they were once cried as slogans, only to be decried later as impossibilities.

If this seems to be imposing too great a concern on those who hold the title to our religious heritage, it needs but to be said, that the idea of freedom itself stems from this cultural matrix. A good many things are to be said about paganism; its virtues—courage, honor, justice, chivalry, etc.—are our own; but some of the great ideas that are germane to our culture, had little if any relevance to certain other cultures. Freedom is only one such ideal value. Not that the pagan precursors of our Western cultural progress had no concept of freedom. That is not true; but such an idea as was held was an indefinite or even apologetic sort of thing. It is interesting to note in this connection that the gods of the Greeks had no patron deity for freedom, while the Roman concession to such divinity was a female figure named Libertas. The classical representation of this less than glamorous lady represented her with a *pileus* in one hand and a laurel wreath in the other. What this is supposed to represent is left to the mythologists to say; but it has a mischievous suggestion that Liberty comes around with her hat in hand, bargaining with a sprig of laurel for the attentions she cannot otherwise win. Maybe it meant that freedom, like the Phoenician cap, could be put on or off at will. Such equivocation in the character of divinity is strange in a pantheon that had furies, fates, muses, gods and goddesses for everything under the sun, each vested with a prerogative and obligation that was as inviolable as it was specific.

However such matters are to be explained, it is fairly obvious that the idea of freedom and its cognates has always been central to our religious culture. The long process of Israel in her achievement of freedom, from the evils of Ur and the slave quarters of Egypt to the lofty moral and spiritual emancipation of Jeremiah and Micah, culminated in the freedom-giving redemption of Jesus and in its elucidation by St. Paul. It was no accident that the first sermon reported of Jesus was concerned with manumission: "The spirit of the Lord is upon me to set at liberty." When the continuing stream of Christian development has kept within this channel, it has scoured deep and flowed with power. On the contrary when it has forgotten or debased its charter of freedom it has meandered, a sluggish and often muddy stream with neither force nor refreshment.

So when the President talks of freedom he is dealing with the heart of Christian culture. This is true whether the freedom under discussion be of speech or religion, or from want or fear. If, furthermore, freedom is a matter of the spirit, not politically derived or maintained, a true understanding of the Four Freedoms is possible only when they are grounded in specific spiritual experiences. It is the melancholy history of other days, that similar slogans built on spiritual sensibilities, have faired ill at the hands of those whose understanding was solely political. Liberty, as Madame Roland's discarnate voice still reminds us, has seen great crimes committed in her name. The possibility that the Four

Freedoms might become the rationale of new tyranny is something to which we must not become blind, and the only way such profanation is to be averted is by a reassertion and reacceptance of freedom as a matter of the spirit. "Stone walls do not a prison make"; that is grammar school sophistication; but that bright slogans may make a cage is something for the wisest to reflect upon all over again.

This is the reason for a book on the Four Freedoms from the standpoint of the Christian faith. The freedom that we dream about must become the discipline we are willing to practice. If we are not willing to be free, it is because we are shackled by what, for the moment, seems more desirable. This is spiritual bondage which no rendezvous at Runnimede or in the North Atlantic can mitigate or manumit. "Where the spirit of the Lord is, there is liberty" [7] is a bold, dogmatic claim. If it seems so to us, what must it have sounded like when read to the small Corinthian fellowship? They knew political servitude and cultural pressure and moral coercion. Presumably also they knew, or came to know liberty even within the constrictions of political, cultural and moral life. The explanation of their liberty was not that pressures were relaxed as a concession to their religious faith. On the contrary. The secret lay in a spirit they possessed.

[7] II Cor. 3:17.

Time changes many things, but the nature of man's spirit and his response to life are not alterable so far as two thousand years have measured. There are many who will gainsay the apostle's use of "the Lord" who will not now demur at the word "spirit." It is the latter word which is, in the present world context, the more important. The "lords" of the world are many and allegiance will be varied and strange; but the spirit of man is of one immutable stuff, however oddly men behave. If the Four Freedoms he seeks are found to be spiritually attainable there is much hope for the world. If they are only politically understood and sought, there is little.

Having set forth the emphasis that will be laid on this discussion of the Four Freedoms, a further preliminary word is to the point. The order in which they are given by the President seems unimportant for, as a matter of fact, they are variously interchanged in his own numerous statements about them. The point to be observed is that they lie in the four dominant areas of human experience. Free religion is necessary to man's aspirational and ethical concerns, free speech is necessary to his social and political interests; without freedom from want a stable and secure material economy is impossible; and without freedom from fear, no creative integration of personality about a center of control is to be achieved. Ethics, sociology, economics, psychology, these describe the areas of man's action. To attempt to get on without any one of them is futile; to accept constraint beyond a certain point in any is to restrict all action unduly. Ethical bondage cuts the nerve of the spirit in personal conduct, social bondage is slavery; economic bondage is destitution; psychological bondage is disintegration. Furthermore when it is put thus, the spiritual aspect of each of these human needs becomes manifest; ethical or religious freedom is not unrestraint but discipline in terms of a spiritual quest; social or political freedom is seen to be possible only where social discipline is voluntarily accepted by the components of society or government; economic freedom can be possible only when and where the spiritual rights of the individual—those rights that inhere in the fact of his being human—are recognized as the basis for his economic rights; psychological freedom which by all odds is the hardest to achieve, comes about only when spiritual disciplines are understood and exercised in the interests of psychological or spiritual integration.

To sum up: This discussion of the Four Freedoms will follow the order as published in *Current History*. It will proceed on the assumption that none of these can be left out of any complete picture of the human struggle, though others might be added. Also that they must be understood in terms of the spirit, if they are to be understood at all. An unfree government is despotism, hence the need for free speech; a fettered religion is superstition or formalism, hence the demand for free religion; a social order in which men are slaves to debt or impoverishment is, to that extent, destitute, hence the necessity for freedom from want; an individual tyrannized by normal fear from whatever cause is held in psychological peonage of the most disintegrative sort, hence the need for freedom from fear. The President says these four liberations are to coextend to all the world. That's a big order. It will take spiritual resourcefulness and resolution past our present computations; but if the goal is worthy, the effort should be engrossing.

*For every kind of beasts, and of birds and of serpents, and
of things in the sea is tamed of mankind:*

*But the tongue can no man tame; it is an unruly evil, full
of deadly poison.*

*Therewith bless we God, even the Father, and therewith
curse we men, which are made after the similitude of God.
. . . . My brethren, these things ought not so
to be.*

Jas. 3: 7-10

*Speech is civilization itself. The word, even the most contra-
dictory word, preserves contact—it is silence which isolates.*

Thomas Mann: *The Magic Mountain*

1

FREEDOM OF SPEECH

*"We are inspired by a faith which goes back through all the
years to the first chapter of the Book of Genesis: God created
man in His own image."*[1]

It may seem a strange thing to say that freedom of
speech has its roots in the Book of Genesis, but such,
upon examination, may prove to be the case. Not that
either of the principals in the Eden episode talked too
freely and to his own hurt. It is more fundamental than
that. For the fact that man is represented in that
delightful legend as being able to talk at all may be

[1] *Op. cit.* President's Address, p. 1.

properly adduced in support of the plausibility of his having been created in the image of God.

To retrace our steps for a moment: all freedom as we know it in the pattern of our Western culture, issues from the Christian matrix. Freedom is the aim of the Christian testimony; salvation is a perfect synonym, redemption is another. Therefore any conception of Christianity that is externally coercive is spurious; worse still, it is not redemptive. It follows therefore that freedom of speech is a basal religious necessity. More than that it is a basal spiritual necessity. If it is true that only as speech is free is politics possible— for politics is action within government based on independent thought and expression—it is equally true that only as speech is free can religion be creative and redemptive.

[1]

What is speech? This is no frivolous question; indeed until we are sure of our answer we cannot discuss whether it should be free or fettered. On its lowest level, speech is one of the ways in which organisms communicate; on its highest level it is God's greatest instrumental endowment to man.

Most organisms can communicate something about themselves to other organisms on their own level. The very fact of the interdependence of all forms of life makes this necessary for survival. By its fragrance one flower communicates at night with the nocturnal insect whose visit helps perform the function of pollenization; by its color another flower invites a different insect during the day. The ant by a quick, delicate contact with his antenna "says" something to his fellow as he meets him; the note of the bird proclaims his right of eminent domain from a tall tree or the urgency he feels for a mate to share his nesting inclinations. Fragrance, color, call, gesture, contact, grimace, all these are communicative devices, the interruption of which for half a springtide would presumably reduce the earth to desolation. The cycle of life depends on it: no flower no seed, no seed no harvest, no harvest no food, no food no life. Along the fragile lines of wordless communication the secret of life is told and the pulse of life is felt.

Civilization is communication with words. That does not say enough except in the present context. The fact that a man can put his basal impulses into words is the primary significance of civilization; and the further fact of the diversity of language is the explanation of the varieties that civilization has shown in the long course of history. Primitive words make for primitive social patterns, elaborate language makes for elaborate culture. We expect the savage who—according to the comics says "glug, glug"—to wear the skins of animals one way; where the ladies wear their animal pelts more fastidiously, we expect their cocktail conversation to effloresce into another kind of verbiage.

The wit who said "monkeys very sensibly refrain from speech lest they be put to work earning man's living" may have gone sour on the way men have conducted themselves, but there is nevertheless wisdom as well as rebuke in his words. Whatever may be one's judgment on the way this endowment of language has been used, it represents man's *potential* superiority over all other organisms. In a very real sense, speech is evidence of the Divine in man. The famous verse in the creation epic might with equal significance read: "And God breathed into his nostrils the breath of life and he became a talking soul." Thus the President goes back to Genesis for his ultimate reason for the freedom of speech.

It is then neither naïveté nor pride that makes us grant the power of speech to something we wish to exalt. So when Shadow, our black cocker spaniel, barks for a piece of candy we pretend he is saying "please" —no slight compliment in a day when polite manners are perhaps less scrupulously observed than formerly. So also the psalmist, rhapsodizing about the bright universe of day and night says: "Day unto day uttereth *speech* and night unto night sheweth knowledge." So also Emerson:

> . . . the bird language rightly *spell*
> And that which roses *say* so well.

It follows then that this unique spiritual endowment (we do not hold with those who say that thought is merely subvocal speech) is to be used not automatically or merely by instinct as the lion's roar or the thrush's note, but subject to spiritual controls for good or ill. We know Voltaire flavored his comments about life with the acid of cynicism so we do not take too seriously his famous sentence: "Men use their thoughts only to justify their wrong doings and employ speech to conceal their thoughts." Nevertheless he attributes to both idea and speech, a moral purpose, or immoral, if you prefer. The usually good-natured Oliver Goldsmith must have quarreled with his wife the day he wrote that "the true use of speech is not so much to express our wants as to conceal them." She had perhaps sought a confession from him that he had parried with a verbal dodge. But he was both wise and witty when he said to Dr. Johnson: "If you were to make little fishes talk, they would talk like whales." A spiritual exercise in self-inflation!

It is the fact of the moral connotation of speech that gives the human method of communication its appalling importance. This is not true of the exchanges between the lesser folk. The love note of a cardinal on his bough, the fragrance of a blossom with a heart dusty with pollen gold, the aromatic warning of *mephitis mephitica* broadcast across the landscape at sunset, these may be lovely or nauseating according to human tastes, but they do not seem to have moral value, and if there is spiritual significance ascribed to them, it is the doing of poets. Yet it is true, literally and disturbingly true, that one can never utter with communicative intent, even a single detached syllable and be sure it will have no moral or spiritual consequence. It is never the case that it makes no difference what one says. On the contrary, it always makes a difference though fortunately most of the time the difference is inconsequential. One word may change the destiny of a nation. One word spoken in an upper room in Jerusalem actually did change the course of human history; it was the smallest of all possible words—I. When Judas Iscariot, in response to the incriminating gesture of the Lord said, with the rising inflection of a question—"I?"—he confirmed in his dark soul the determination of betrayal. The world has never been the same since.

Recognition of the moral quality that inheres in every word spoken with the intention of conveying an idea has been general, and it is basal to any understanding of what freedom of speech is. The copybook maxim

> Boys flying kites haul in their white-winged birds:
> You cannot do that when you're flying words.

recognizes that one word may make the difference between conflict and communion, between security and strife. Martin Luther said the overthrow of the Prince of Darkness could be accomplished by one word: "one little word can fell him." The psalmist urging that the heart be kept from evil and the lips from speaking guile was warning against the evil potential in every guileful word.

[2]

If what has been said is the proper answer to the question: What is speech? we are now in a position to inquire what freedom of speech is. While one may use language freely as "monkey chatter underneath the moon," one cannot speak words in the hope that no moral responsibility will attach to them. No one should ever say anything under the illusion that it doesn't make any difference what one says. To a morally sensitive spirit such irresponsibility is a misuse both of intelligence and language and—what is more serious— it is dangerous. It is this latter fact that has made it necessary to restrict speech under certain circumstances.

It makes a good deal of difference who it is that regards what is dangerous. With spectacular severity the dictators of the modern world abrogate *all* freedom of *all* speech, because all speech to the tyrant is as potentially dangerous as all freedom. The jest is silenced with the jibe; laughter is forbidden along with the complaint. This is the ultimate in terror of which we, in experience, know little. But even democratic states that cherish and encourage freedom of speech realize that under certain circumstances, limits are properly set to the things that can be said. Such circumstances, while very often dramatized in a political context are always essentially moral, and that is only another way of saying that the extent of the freedom our speech is to enjoy is primarily a spiritual measurement. That democratic states sometimes feel the necessity of imposing restraint on speech with an apologetic and cautious mandate, is a further evidence of the spiritual background of all such action.

It would seem, then, that the spiritual quality of a given period largely—if indeed not entirely—determines the extent of freedom of speech. Tranquil times are spiritually hospitable to the tolerance and leisure of debate. Ideally under such conditions, Congress, for example, could indulge the dubious luxury of endless argument or even of filibuster. But should the sergeant-at-arms invade such an idyllic forensic Eden with the announcement that the Capitol building was on fire, none would object to the temporary total abridgment of the rights of free speech by the speaker.

But in turbulent times, when the souls of men are as uncertain as their material fortunes, when one word may tip the balance from normal risk to extraordinary danger there is always a tendency to exercise greater control than is perhaps necessary or advisable. At that point the use of one's moral prerogative of free speech passes from a personal right to a moral responsibility. And only those who are spiritually sensitive to this moral question will rightly speak or keep silence. The problem ceases to be academic in the terrible urgency of the need for averting the imminent peril. So when, as always in stressful times, we hear a debate concerning the censorship of news between those who, at one extreme, claim the absolute right and duty to say anything, anywhere, at any time, to anybody; and those at the other extreme who refuse the right of anyone to speak anything with uncompromising directness, we seem to hear the noise of an argument predicated primarily on political presuppositions. This is not to say that politics has no inherent moral reference; it is to say that the aim of most democratic political argument is the acquisition of power within and by means of group action. Where power is the primary necessity, the potency of evil as well as of good is equally sought and used as the political means in its achievement.

[3]

Freedom of speech will always be something to make a fuss about within a democratic society, and its solution in terms of politics will be reached always in terms of political power. This is true in our own country; it will be even more so when we begin extending the application of the principle of free speech "everywhere throughout the world," as the President has put it. The postwar world will be a terrible confusion for a while until power is consolidated in the hands of those who can use it to restore order. This does not make much room for the preachments of the free-speech advocates. It is not a comforting prospect, but what is to happen for a generation in the rest of the world does not invite any very great hope that freedom of speech will be anything but a slogan, dimly heard by millions whose first concern inevitably will be with food of any sort instead of freedom of any kind.

It is this fear that the appalling postwar situation will turn this great spiritual concept of freedom of speech— spiritual because of the very nature of language as our human means of communication—into a slogan and invite the distrust and disillusionment that all dead slogans have visited upon them, that we are calling for an understanding of the matter in terms of the human spirit. Not that such an approach will infallibly keep the idea vital and creative; but that turning it over to the hypodermic injections of politicians will certainly only sustain it fitfully if at all, allowing it alternately long moribund intervals during one of which it may finally die. Is there anything to be found within the Christian tradition that is suggestive? Put it otherwise: what has the church to say about freedom of speech for the whole world?

This question is, we are convinced, quite within the proper area of Christian concern, since every word spoken with a view of communicating an idea has moral connotations and therefore involves moral responsibilities. Moral responsibility rests lightly on those who demand ultimate rights even for irresponsible speech. Similarly it is denied by those who permit no freedom at all. A morally sensitive religion should have or should seek a standard by which the quality and extent of all freedom and restraint should be judged. There should be such a standard irrespective of the character of the group within which freedom is exercised or denied. And the possibility of such a norm derives from the essential oneness of the human spirit, in spite of the apparent variety of group life patterns.

The idea of the freedom of speech was not new when the Christian testimony began to take shape in the first century. God, according to the ancients in Israel, had what is perhaps the only real freedom of speech of which man has thought. "He uttered his word and the earth melted." That is not a geologist's report of volcanic disturbance; it is a concession by a morally sensitive man that if God wanted to, He had the right to speak freely even if His language proved to be inflammatory in the most literal sense. Yet this concession to deity did not carry over to those who regarded themselves as His spokesmen. When they said, as the credential of their words, "thus saith the Lord," they hazarded all the risks that attend speech spoken to hostile listeners. They had to accept the consequences of their words and they did so. Actuated by a sense of high moral responsibility, they, at the same time claimed no exemption from the results of their forthrightness. Elijah dared to face Ahab and Jezebel, but he knew, while he was speaking Jehovah's threat, that there was a hide-out on the Brook Kerith whither he could flee, if the pursuit were not too hot or the pace too fast.

These prophets in the great tradition of Israel were not politically minded. There were, to be sure, politicians in Israel; but they were not a part of the small fellowship of honor and certitude that believed that God alone had the right to power and that those who sought it for themselves, struggled verily against the high God. The prophets were therefore less concerned with their power than with what they conceived was God's will. This was a great spiritual dynamic; it was of that quality of spirit that always and alone produced prophets.

Their confidence stemmed from two great spiritual certainties: they were sure that God's will was going to prevail in human affairs; they were sure that what God wanted to say, Israel needed to hear. Because of the former they could abjure the struggle for power the politicians carried on; because of the latter they could sit in judgment on the human struggle for power and speak thunderingly against it, accepting the consequences with fortitude and even with hilarity.

The experience of Jesus is similarly instructive. We shall see, as we get on, that his experience of freedom gave freshness to all his contacts with life in the areas of religion, government, the supply of physical needs and the banishment of fear. In the present context we need only to point out that in a singular way he felt the release that we call freedom of speech amid the constrictions that formalism had laid upon independent speaking in his day. There is no question that such freedom of speech as was allowed in Palestine was not enjoyed by the natives. The chances are that it was even grudgingly conceded to the hirelings of Rome. The crust of formalism that had formed upon the religion of Israel had, for the most part, killed off the prophetic impulse. Where that is dead, freedom of speech is wholly academic. Such rebellion against Rome's tyranny as flared out from time to time was political, sporadic and inconclusive. The Zealots cared less for concessions to their tongues than to their wish to rule themselves.

And yet Jesus spoke with freedom that was sometimes little short of rashness. He was, indeed, ostensibly killed for what He said, though his words about the destruction of the temple and its restoration after three days were interpreted politically when to him they had spiritual reference exclusively. The reason and norm for his unfettered utterance was no different, however, from that of the prophets before him. Except for this important difference: he had a sharper sense of the invincible power of the human spirit and of its final right to judge both the speech and action of men. The spirit bloweth where it listeth. We hear the sound thereof and know not whither it cometh or whither it goeth. So also is everyone that is born of the spirit. Because his sense of freedom was analogous to his sense of spiritual power, he spoke as he wanted to and "no man ever spake as this man spake."

Yet all the while this impulse of spiritual freedom spoke under the great prophetic assurance that God's will would surely prevail; and that what God wanted to say, Israel needed to hear. No law of Rome and no precept of the temple could deny him that right. This was not irresponsibility, neither was it freedom of speech politically prescribed; it was freedom of speech in terms of the spirit, and it was the spirit that both extended and retracted the liberty as the case appeared to be.

[4]

The confidence of the Christian fellowship in these basic and controlling spiritual principles of free speech is not particularly vigorous today. Why this is so is not our present concern. But this is fairly certain: if those who give lip service to the idea of spiritual values—and we have noted an increasing boldness in some writers to affirm this fact—should allow spiritual constraints to determine what they say as to what God wants as it is related to what man needs, they would certainly speak with greater wisdom and greater restraint. The practical result would be to make them—we might properly say us—face in advance the moral consequences of our words, that quality that gives speech its uniqueness and its terrifying power. It would also lend gravity to our words and at the same time reduce their hazard.

But obviously those who are most concerned with the problem of the freedom of speech are impatient with the idea of spiritual controls. Those who recognize them speak with greater clarity; those who don't, make the louder noise. It is this circumstance that points up the importance of the President's promise at this time. There is a prodigious task of educating the world in the spiritual bases of freedom, as different from, and often opposing its political bases. In the interests of world-wide democracy he has promised it to all who have lost it or who never had it. In the interests of democracy at home he has, by the same token, made it important for us to keep a moral as well as a legal right to it. From the standpoint of the Christian church this is a proposal of exciting importance. Why?

We have said that in the body of the Christian tradition, God alone has the right of absolute freedom of speech. Such language may be obscure, but its metaphorical import is easy. It follows then that those who are spiritually sensitive to the moral implications of all language will set for themselves certain restraints that arise, not out of the context of political struggle but out of the sense of moral responsibility. Since political pressures are likely to be more powerful and explicit, it will be easier to accept political restraints than those laid upon us by our own inner sense of obligation. And yet it is the latter sort of restraint that is the higher. It calls, therefore, for high spiritual standards and delicate spiritual sensitivity. The former may be put in the pattern of an axiom: Whatever is true is good; the latter can be described in a proposition: Before one speaks what he believes to be true he will consult his inner monitor as well as his legal rights. These two matters call for brief elucidation.

First as to the axiom: Whatever is true is good. This has venerable and profound support; it has been the core of what the spiritually sensitive have been saying for twenty-five hundred years; and it is the politically sensitive who have denied it. The Plato who believed it was Plato the philosopher, not Plato the politician.

We remember that when he turned politico he missed
being sold into actual physical slavery only by the quick
wit of an opulent friend who perhaps thought Plato
had learned his lesson and retrieved him for more
important business than governing Syracuse. There is
no heresy so base as that which says truth may turn
out to be bad. It carries in its ruin the fear that good
may turn out to be evil. To consent to either proposition
is to clear the political arena for the unrestricted opera-
tions of the opportunist and the cynic. But to assent to
the axiom is only the start of a spiritual discipline. It is
quite possible to agree that the palatability of a fact
has no relation to its importance and go on to the
mistaken notion that the unpalatability of a fact is a
demand for its immediate proclamation. Between the
two lies a segment of spiritual discipline that cannot
be detoured. And this means that the speaker must be
spiritually literate. Quite properly the brochure issued
on the Four Freedoms by the O.W.I. says:

Certain favorable conditions are necessary before freedom of speech acquires validity. The first condition is that,
the individual have something to say. Literacy is a pre-
requisite of free speech, and gives it point.

This means more, in our view, than the ability to read
the papers. Unhappily that is not always the most
direct route to spiritual and moral literacy. For us it
means a spiritual literacy that comes solely by discipline

exercised under the direction of the inner monitor. Those who endanger the moral validity of the principle of free speech are not the unhappy few who cannot read; they are the unhappy majority—one fears—who are spiritually unlearned. It is the man who believes that truth is good—the children of Israel put it in terms of the righteous will of Jehovah—and who has, by spiritual disciplines discovered what *is* good, who has a right to speak freely.

Before the social criterion is discussed it may well be confessed at this point that the belief that spiritual discipline produces a moral consensus lies at the heart of the position maintained here. If we are to escape chaos in our ultimate understanding of the nature of man and society, we must seek it in the direction of an integrated spiritual order informing the nature of things. This does not mean "spiritual mechanism" as some have caricatured it, or the denial of man's essential individuality. Rather does it indicate that the universe being what it is and man's spirit being a part of the infinite plexus, his spirit, in quest of truth for action will find it, will find it good, and will find that his fellow questers have also found it.

But there are social complications involved. For this reason, added to our axiom, we must have a principle of action. It is a variant of the statement above to say that the spiritually sensitive free-speaker will seek to discover not only what the truth for action is, but to what extent his speaking will benefit other individuals —both those who are and who are not under spiritual discipline—and society as a whole.

This is a big order, but then the President has set us forth on an enterprise which expands in every direction no matter how we turn. And yet such a discipline is, in other terms, very close kin to the exercise of good taste. Indeed so speaks the O.W.I. brochure: "Good taste sets limits on all speech." That certainly ought to be the case, and what better results should spiritual discipline achieve than that fine quality of spirit which we call good taste? And, to refer to another familiar way of putting it, the three famous questions long since designed to restrain the gossip's tongue, set the obligation up neatly. Before one speaks one should ask: Is it true; is it kind; is it necessary? The gossip may, presumably, move over to accommodate all of us who say things, and with immense profit to us all.

[5]

Herein appears what to some is a part of the obligation of the Christian fellowship during these days. The church has been both despotic and democratic in its history, and its record, regarding the freedom of speech, both within itself and within the larger context of society, has been spotty. In fact, the chances are that save for the present-day denial of the right of free speech by the Axis powers, the record of the church is more humiliating than that of any government, *per se.* The principle of free speech provides that one may "talk—not without fear of contradiction, but without fear of punishment," as the O.W.I. puts it. Alas that the church has—and be it shamefully confessed still does—not only contradicted, but has punished, and its penalties have been even more enduring and terrifying than its contradictions. The firing squad is bad enough, but eternal damnation, for those who fear it, is worse.

At the same time the church has also been the proving ground for the ideal and practice of free speech. This is the essence of the prophetic spirit as it has extended, not—as Voltaire said of the origin of religion —that it began when the first knave met the first fool, but from the point where the first prophet met the first publican. The church has the right to speak freely only when it, through its own inner disciplines, has kept spiritually sensitive and morally responsive to all the implications of its place and action in society. This means that it must abjure such political pretensions as it may have cherished; and this, primarily for the reason that when it makes use of political expedients, it accepts political morals, and that involves, as already indicated, the opportunistic use of both good and evil in the quest for power. As this applies to freedom of speech its places the church in the position of conceding the right only if it expedites its campaign for power. Conversely, and implemented with threats of endless torment for the dissident, it can deny the right as forthrightly as predatory political fascism.

Ideally however, the church should be the place for the demonstration of the practice of freedom of speech. It is ethically sensitive and morally responsive to the implications of freedom. Furthermore its interest is primarily related to the quest and dissemination of truth. The redemptive forth-telling of such truth as she has is possible in such proportion as she has no institutional ax to grind.

Can it then claim of the state, protection in its right to speak freely on any matter so long as it aims not for its own advantage or power, but is concerned for the well-being of both society and the individual? The state has shown a minimum of concern for withdrawing freedom of speech from the pulpit in our country. This is true in spite of the fact that abroad the pulpit was put under surveillance at once by the fascists. European politicians know the pulpit's power and the pulpit's peril. The tradition of a free pulpit as it has survived one hundred and fifty years of every sort of sect and aberration among us makes us little apprehensive that the tradition will, even under the most intolerable provocation, be abrogated here. But should the church expect the state to continue the concession if within the church itself the concession is withdrawn?

Here is a new threat that we may do well to face before it grows to more sizable dimensions. The present world struggle has produced a few instances in which churches have to all intents and purposes expelled their ministers for their espousal of causes that were, for the moment, unpopular. It may be democratic to vote the ministerial office vacant. By the same token it may be democratic to vote to withdraw from the minister his right to speak freely. The point of our whole discussion, however, turns on the maintenance of this essential freedom at all costs, not on the wisdom of its abrogation by certain respectable expedients. There is a conflict sure to follow the end of the military phase of the current world revolution. One of its opening stratagems will be to suggest deviously that the pulpit be kept silent. The native fascists of church, industry and government are growing increasingly bold in their predictions about what is to happen, and that of which they are most certain is that the voices likely to oppose them in the church, will in one way or another be muted. This is, of course, only another manifestation of the political struggle for power of which so much has already been said. If then, for any reason under heaven, the church fails, within itself, to keep its pulpits free, it shall deserve—and perhaps get—the repressive measures that have been invoked upon it elsewhere.

This is why the church rightly feels that its prerogative to criticize the moral issues in the present world revolution must be kept inviolate so long as its utterance is spiritually derived. Some have lamented what is called the strange moral obtuseness of certain churchmen on current war issues. Moral shilly-shallying, it has been termed. Is it not, however, quite the contrary? Moral issues have been *so* clear to some of the church's leaders that they have stood their ground, refusing to be coerced into the dubious business of war-absolving. It is that they have refused to shilly-shally that has annoyed some who want them to reflect the change of every vagrant wind by a quick and decisive shift of their own position.

[6]

It was Wordsworth who, slightly more than a century ago, wrote:

> We must be free or die who speak the tongue
> That Shakespeare spoke, the faith and morals hold
> Which Milton held.

He seems to be talking about two different things, but for our present purpose we may think of him as having said: We who speak the language Shakespeare spoke are free to use it only under the guidance of the faith and morals Milton held, or we will die. Now, according to the President, the concession is to be guaranteed far beyond those who speak the tongue of Shakespeare. It extends to the language of Confucius, Peter the Great and the Grand Lama. It will take so long to recreate these alien masses into political bodies that will guarantee freedom of speech that the prospect daunts us. But the Christian enterprise has been busy all over the world for centuries nurturing the spiritual appetency that gives to freedom of speech its ultimate sanction and validity. This is not far from claiming that the President's proclamation is a new missionary mandate. Indeed our study of all four of the freedoms will lead us to that inescapable obligation.

So the Christian church must exercise freedom of speech, both as norm and example to the world that is in the making. If within the Christian fellowship this demonstration is not made, where else will it be made? Not, we fear, in parliaments for they can be silenced where the church cannot be. And if no demonstration is made, how will the practice of free speech be encouraged? Not by proclamation in pacts and charters alone. And if free speech is not encouraged, it may die; and if it dies we shall have started backward down the long road that leads to the chattering of apes, or the silent communication between flower and bird. That will mean we have begun to lose God's great instrumental endowment, that gift by which we have learned to communicate with our fellows, and with Him. And if we lose that, civilization will follow us into the jungle, and the race of man will pass into the muted silences of spiritual darkness.

Freedom of speech indeed! Let us by all means make it available to all the world, but while we prepare for its export, we must be doubly sure what it is, and see to it that the supply we have will not be exhausted here by its distribution abroad.

*Pure religion and undefiled before God and the Father is
this, to visit the fatherless and widows in their affliction and
to keep Himself unspotted from the world.*

JAS. 1:27

*Religion is a great force—the only real motive force in the
world; but what you fellows don't understand is that you must
get at a man through his own religion and not through yours.*

GEORGE BERNARD SHAW: *Getting Married*

2

FREEDOM OF RELIGION

*"That there is a crisis in the Christian church and in the
Christian faith is undeniable. The World War that rages over
the entire globe had its origins in Christendom, in the West,
where for centuries two irreconcilable spirits have laid claim
to man: that of force, and that of Christianity."* [1]

Miss Thompson was thinking of Christmas as she
wrote her column for December 23, 1942. That the
return of the festival always invites the attention of
newspaper pundits to such matters as the above quotation touches, is all to the good; that such reflections
are generally tossed out with the tinsel after the holidays
is all to the bad, for the reason that our world illness
is primarily spiritual. Thus Miss Thompson again from
the same column:

[1] Dorothy Thompson, "On the Record," (Bell Syndicate)
December 23, 1942.

. . . the whole of our civilization is sick for a living ethos [ethos is borrowed from the Greek word meaning simply "character." It seems to be used here as a synonym for religion as it supplies moral purpose.] Its experiments and adjustments fail for the lack of an integrating faith . . . a society that, in the main currents of its life has no strong imperatives of good and evil . . . and in which no vital faith burns brightly throughout all its parts cannot bring order out of chaos with even the most brilliant formulas.

[1]

This brings our discussion sharply to the question of the freedom of religion. In the previous chapter it has been argued that freedom of speech must be based on what Miss Thompson describes aptly as "strong imperatives of good and evil," and a "vital faith" which "burns brightly throughout all its (society's) parts." This strong imperative has been presented as a spiritual urgency, a sense of moral responsibility that is rudimentary in the nature of human speech, an urgency therefore that is prior to the political situations which, on the basis of what is expedient to the struggle for power, determine the extent to which the right to speak freely is conceded or withheld. The church, it has been argued, because ideally it is sensitive to spiritual things, and able—also ideally—to exhibit the true moral nature of the freedom of speech, has an important obligation in the present struggle; namely, to encourage "strong imperatives of good" within society, and to demonstrate within its own fellowship the moral worth of this first-named freedom in the President's foursome. Thus the genuine article can be produced according to standard specifications (the standard is clear in the Judeo-Christian prophetic tradition) and in such sufficient amount as will make its export abroad possible.

We have been wholly within the wide field of religion as we have discussed the freedom of speech; nor shall we be able to range beyond the limits of religion in anything that will be said—another way of emphasizing the essentially spiritual nature of our world revolution. Manifestly then, religion itself must be free; and yet it is not easy to achieve for it so lofty a status. This arises partly out of the circumstance that high religion demands the uttermost in one's loyalty, and the very intensity of one's finest devotion acts legitimately as a constraint more arbitrary than chains.

Before tackling the problem, let it be noted in passing that the peril of sloganizing hangs about this elevated ideal also. Speech is God's first instrumental endowment to man, we have said. Religion, it may be added, is man's highest use of his finest endowment. The mystery of prayer—and it is very great—lies in the fact that prayer is, in one way or another, communicating freely with God. That finite man can hold communion with infinite Being is the basal assumption of prayer; it is also that which is quite impossible to prove, since empirical evidence for the alleged crossings back and forth between finitude and infinity is hard to come by if indeed it is to be had at all. If we were sure philosophically that there is such interchange between these two worlds ("world" is unclear—"two worlds" is confusing, but what language can be precise in dealing with mystery?), and empirically certain that we had accomplished it, religion would be the most natural and most free of all possible human exercises. We must be as vigilant therefore in the case of free religion as in the case of free speech to keep the discussion from falling to the slogan level. Furthermore, because it is more acutely dangerous, we must not allow the crusade for free religion to become a political expedient. It is not always realized but it is frequently true, that efforts to win freedom for religion, end up in making a religion of freedom. There are those who worship freedom. Unhappily for many their derivative deity turns easily into a devil. In Hitler's vocabulary it is unwittingly called *Lebensraum,* and what orgies its worship has inspired.

[2]

Our discussion will lead us along lines suggested by four questions: What is religion? Why should it be free? What is it that imprisons religion? How can its release from its bonds be accomplished? It is within the orbit of these four inquiries that the problem of the freedom of religion lies. If we cannot be sure that we have free religion, it is, of course, perversity to propose that we can guarantee it everywhere in the world.

What is religion? The O.W.I., for its own limited purposes puts the answer thus:

. . . a source of moral values which transcends the immediate necessities of the community, however important these may be. It is one thing to pay taxes to the state—this men will do; it is another to submit their consciences to the state—this they politely decline. The wise community respects this mysterious quality in the individual, and makes its plans accordingly.

This is an admirable, and in some respects, a daring statement for an official bureau to make in wartime, and is so clear as to require no analysis. It needs, however, to be pointed out, that if that is what religion is, religion, by the very nature of the human spirit, is indefeasibly free—as free in a Nazi concentration camp as in a Quaker meeting. The "mysterious quality in the individual" is mysterious because it escapes rationalization—which is imprisonment in ideas. In other words "the mysterious quality" is the quality of freedom, and no shackles, whether snapped shut by the Gestapo, or forged by the sense of fellowship in devotion, can confine it. This would seem to lift the freedom of religion out of the category of a problem or a world-wide desideratum, and establish it as something already achieved everywhere by the very nature of the human spirit. Unhappily this is not the case. There is still the problem at home, and the need for its achievement in the rest of the world.

What is religion? There is a compilation of definitions which, when last scrutinized yielded the amazing total of twelve hundred answers to the question. That was ten years ago and it is reasonably certain that the definition makers and compilers have not been idle during the past decade. The list may have been doubled by now and have become so complete as to satisfy the most fastidious. Indeed saint and sinner, extrovert and neurotic, monk and blasphemer could, in all likelihood prove, by pointing out the definition of their choice, that they were all pious men.

We shall add no new definition to this compendium. Hard cases make bad laws, warns the jurist; hard sinners, for the same reason, make bad definitions of religion. Yet religion is, after all, essentially simple, and we do well to trust the simple definitions of universal experience. Actually it is only universal experience that can be simply defined; the more unique the event, the more elaborate the description. Thus viewed, religion is man's effort to establish and sustain contact with the object of his highest devotion or value, be it a lover, a status, a dollar, a star, or a painted stick. It is man's "effort to establish" because true religion is not a static or finally achieved status, and also because true religion is functional—a life, a career, not a creed or an institution or a record. Jesus, whose minimum claim to fame rests on his having been the founder of a religion, called his work the business of making more abundant life available; and Paul whose fame rests—among other claims—on his formulations of the Christian idea and ethic said: "It is the spirit that giveth life."

That this primitive human experience, for such it is —establishing contact with one's highest value—has expanded to the widest periphery of human experience is the reason why definitions of religion can be so numerous and at the same time so true. The cave man who propitiated the storm or the flame was afraid, and yet that fear was commingled with admiration for power. His religion was a compound, one element of which was a search for a value that for the moment was dangerous because he had not learned the knack of proper contact. There is a wide interval in time and in the visible aspects of the mass, separating the cringing savage and the genuflecting priest, but the impulse that animates each is the same. Ultimately therefore freedom of the impulse can be smothered only by the externals of worship, the routines of institution or the rubrics of creed, fashioned for its own use. The *impulse* to propitiate or parade can never be imprisoned. It can be vitiated or dissipated by the accessories of worship, or atrophied through neglect, but upon the primitive impulse no shackles can be forged.

It is irrelevant therefore to ask whether religion should or should not be free since by its nature it *is* free. Thomas Paine was right in saying that liberty to worship God could no more be granted a man than freedom to accept it could be granted God. One might as well confer the right of a bird to fly or a mother to caress her baby.

It is not religion in its essence that is threatened from without, and against which the President speaks. As an institution it takes its chances along with all other social enterprises, and its fortunes flourish or decline with most other social structures. It is rather concerning the trespass on the secondary aspects of religion that our interest is to be engaged if we are to follow the Executive lead. He says religion is not free and must be liberated everywhere. It is easy to see that there is a recrudescence of religious persecution in parts of the Western world, notably in Russia where it may have been deserved—if persecution can ever be extenuated. Savagely has the Gestapo set about to stamp it out in Germany, and it is this circumstance added to the threat of an extension of suppression around the world that has roused a shocked world to go to war against it.[2] We

[2] This is by no means to be taken as a statement of the cause of the present war. It would be incredibly naïve to believe

of the West, where tolerance is often indistinguishable from smugness, had good reason to be aroused at such official acts against the clergy and communicants of long-established religious groups. We thought the world was through with that. We recall with shame the disgraceful witch hunts of Salem; indeed we have developed a sort of posthumous fondness for the victims commensurate with our post-mortem scorn of the pious perpetrators. Missionaries were once eaten in the Solomons; to the Chinese they were foreign devils, as to the cannibals they were long pig. Blandly we assumed that because the Chinese of late have withheld the epithet and the cannibals have returned to more decorous fare, the Christian West could not possibly see the return of the rack, the gibbet and the auto-da-fé within our own generation. Since we have given over burning religious heretics, reserving the heat of our anger for political witches and radicals, we are scandalized by the sadism of Jew-baiting and its correlative horrors. But here it is—religion unfree and, worse by far, persecuted.

Yet we are not inhospitable to the whisperings of self-righteousness that subtly advise us that a religion in bondage, as in Europe, is something that cannot happen here. Europe's institutions, Europe's creeds, Europe's

America was moved to a declaration of war by the rise of German neopaganism or the imprisonment of Neimöller and what that stood for.

vital faiths are decadent, we say condescendingly. No doors are padlocked today against our entrance into the house of God, no secret police skulk to catch the incriminating sound of a radio sermon. Religion is free in America, we boast. Therefore the problem before us is limited to the simple detail of getting the rest of the world to behave as we do.

This would be very reassuring if it were true. Dorothy Thompson, however, seems not quite so sure. There is, she syndicates, a crisis in the church and in the Christian faith; no vital faith burns brightly throughout all its parts. Is this due to a struggle between faith and infidelity the issue of which, being in doubt, leaves partisans without a victor to follow? If there is no vital faith, is it possible that faith is dead? In either case, that of an unresolved struggle or a moribund faith, religion cannot be called free, whatever else is to be said about it. A dead faith might, by the cynic, be regarded as a faith mercifully freed from its integument of superstition, but dead faith is hardly free religion. One is crowded to the confession that while governments abroad have fettered religion by fiat for political reasons, religion at home has been imprisoned by subtler forces as an accommodation to spiritual indolence or intellectual pride.

If we are to export the spirit that liberates religion, we must have it here first. And it cannot be gainsaid that scores of thousands among us have lost their freedom of religion—religion that is the effort to establish and maintain contact with the God who is the acknowledged object of Christian devotion. Effort and contact have been as truly lost as if churches had been barricaded by sandbags and guarded by Storm Troopers. Not that we are not externally free, for we are; but that the spirits of millions in our midst are thrall to turnkeys into whose hands they themselves have put the keys that imprison them.

In dealing with this aspect of the matter it is necessary to say that the advocacy of religion in America has sometimes been the cause of its repudiation. We still think that the man who repudiates religion (of our simple definition) has made himself a prisoner to something else—to irreligion perhaps, or to sophistication. However, it is necessary for the good of our souls to concede that many advocates of religion while sincere have been stupid, while shrewd, have been guilty of hypocrisy, while enthusiatic, have been strained to misemphasis and folly. Nevertheless this is no new thing under the sun; and if it were possible for the aggregate of the ineptitude of the saints to be piled heaven-high for all the world to see, it would still not be high enough to affright a single soul's honest quest for the Eternal. What is religion—what is the significance of God indeed—if not the strong fortress of the human spirit?

Not as a citadel into which one can escape from life, but as a base of spiritual supply from which one organizes and prosecutes one's struggle.

[3]

These warders who hold the keys of our spiritual prisons, who are they?

Social Respectability is one of them. We still await the research of a competent and objective historian aided by a social psychologist who will explain adequately this amazing phenomenon. There are very few individuals who do not think of themselves as religious and feel a certain pride in it. But their fear that others may think they are religious is equally real and rather terrifying. Their religion is a humble and self-effacing thing; they will not wear it on their "sleeve for daws to peck at." Yet if another of their reticent sort speaks forth suddenly in confession of his secret, they rejoice openly. How many such men did the gallant Captain Rickenbacker thrill with his recent unexpected testament of faith? And yet, in what are regarded as highly respectable circles, if a man who "belongs" talks about religion his mind is thought to have been unhinged momentarily by a tragic experience, or he has become cranky in his advance toward old age. One simply doesn't talk about religion! Indeed it is a part of the code of respectability not to talk about anything that represents more than a casual devotion. Mr. Respectable will always speak with great circumspectness and modesty about his business, his wife, his golf score, his bank account. Less then about his religion which lies hidden deep from the glance of nonchalant eyes. So he will rationalize his failure to support organized religion as preoccupation with realistic and immediate affairs. He will even feel that a man in his social stratum who methodically takes time out for the cultivation of his spiritual inclinations, for definite religious devotion and discipline, is either a hypocrite or a half-wit. All the while, however, he is secretly proud that he has a religion of his own—*sui generis,* he is likely to describe it, as though he had carefully put it together without the meddling of priest or St. Paul. Little does he realize that what has actually taken place is that he has turned over to Social Respectability the key that has locked up his religion. It may not be set free until some convulsion shakes the prison. Is this not an explanation of the spate of religious testimonies that the war has already let loose? There comes a time, soon or late, in nearly every life, when tragedy or triumph snatches the key out of the warder's hand and a man's quest for God suddenly breaks into the open. Religion will not be free among us until the tyranny of a coveted status in society is dispossessed of its power to keep us in bondage.

There is another guard that pickets our souls—Intellectual Respectability is his name, and he knows, oddly enough, a good deal about finesse in dealing with careless professors. Here is a circumstance even more puzzling than the one above to which historian and social psychologist were directed. It is not hard to see how preoccupation with the business of making a living, or the necessity of keeping up with the Joneses, can preempt the otherwise normal religious impulses of the human spirit. Such matters are on the fringes of what is really germane to our culture. Business is something we have to have, social climbing is what we like to do, but Western culture in its rich and indestructible essence was not born of finance and formals. It was taken from the three great cultural lodes of Greek, Roman, and Hebrew life and thought, and fused into the new alloy which we, until recently, have unblushingly claimed as the ultimate in philosophical, administrative, and ethical development. Now we are fighting to preserve it, we say.

How then does it come about that campuses in America are the prison houses of religion? The word is hardly too severe, for Intellectual Respectability has by a device more successful among intelligentsia than shackles, bound religion over to a condition which at best is to be called probation or parole, and at worst, ignominy. This is not true in all institutions, but it is true in many of those which claim for themselves the highest rating in objectivity, progressivism and the liberal mind.

Here is the strange thing about it: the element, historically and empirically which has, more than any other, shaped the culture of the West is the Hebrew-Christian ethical tradition. To claim this is not to disparage the Greek and Roman contributions; it is to say what in every other connection is obvious, namely that the basal element in any culture is ethical. Without what Dorothy Thompson calls "strong imperatives of good and evil" no society can cohere. Similarly Herbert Agar in *A Time for Greatness* says our current confusion comes from our failure to recognize that we are morally adrift. It is not a bad economic order, says he, that has upset the balance of the world, it is bad behavior. This may be far from a complete statement, but it puts a needed emphasis on a needed point. Our morals are Hebrew-Christian morals. It makes little difference whether we like the code or its ethical implications. We are then, in the midst of an anti-Christian revolt, and insofar as our culture is one-third Christian in origin—to be statistical about it—our revolt is one-third anti-cultural. Yet many institutions where our culture is understood and taught are as shy of religion as if it were a fake fossil. Academically it is nodded to; it is set up as something one may respect as one respects a professor emeritus; but if an instructor be so ingenuous as to exhibit a genuine orientation toward God, many of his colleagues will think him emotional or atavistic. It is easy for a department head to lift an eyebrow in annoyance, or a junior professor to curl a lip in scorn at one who believes and says that personal religion is as vital to culture as the Code of Justinian or the philosophy of Plato. This does not confuse personal religion with the objective knowledge of the Code of Platonism. It is to say that religion simply does not have the place in a study of culture that it deserves. It is undeniably true that a teacher of religion should have the sort of enthusiasm for his subject that a Platonist is supposed to have for his; it is similarly true that the status of such a teacher is rarely as high in the campus consensus as is that of the philosopher. Lewis Mumford in a timely essay in the *Atlantic* accuses American education of being tribalistic. Tribalism is the state of mind that regards one's own culture as alone important and looks on all other cultures as incidental or fortuitous. Hence he says we are taught the magnificence of our Western cultural inheritance, and all but completely ignore the great cultures of other lands that not only antedate our own, but in some respects are likely to outlast it. The situation with reference to religion is somewhat parallel though it moves in the opposite direction. We are likely to learn more about other religions than our own in some colleges, the result being that many students develop a natural distrust of the validity and importance of the Hebrew-Christian ethical imperative. The college that could require a course in comparative religions would offer a required course in the ethics of Jesus with great trepidation. Professor Bush of Harvard writing recently in the magazine of the Phi Beta Kappa fraternity said:

Throughout the past, until fairly recent times, teachers of literature thought of themselves as above all, teachers of virtue and religion. . . . It is only through such a positive ideal, through the recapture of the humanistic tradition of pedagogy that we can combat the specious attractions of the educationist's gold bricks and train the next generation of citizens and writers so that, in Miltonic language, they may not, in a dangerous fit of the commonwealth, be such poor, shaken, uncertain reeds, of such a tottering conscience, as many of our late counsellors have lately shown themselves, but pillars of the state.

What is more necessary to an understanding of the present struggle than the record that sets forth the ancient dichotomy, for it is ageless, that Miss Thompson describes at the head of this chapter: "two irreconcilable spirits that lay claim to man: that of force and that of Christianity (religion)."

This is what is meant by saying that Intellectual Respectability has turned a key upon the freedom of religion. The results of this are seen in the appalling spiritual illiteracy of many otherwise intelligent people. Yet we have a religious tradition in a literary compendium which, from the first chapter of Genesis to the closing words of the Revelation, contains a total insight into the psychology of man and the philosophy of God unparalleled in any literature. This is not special pleading for a book that has been caricatured both by its friends and its enemies. It is to claim for the Bible a respect due to any deposit of cultural profundity and beauty; a resource of understanding concerning which the Western world is becoming dangerously unschooled.

[4]

This is disquieting enough in all conscience, but a situation has arisen that is even more disturbing. Within the past six months the status of liberal education as we have known it for two hundred years or more has been imperiled by the usurpation of schools and colleges by the military for training the new armies the times seem to demand. President Seymour of Yale said recently in the New York *Times* magazine that liberal education as we have known it is finished. One assumes he meant for the duration, but the comment of a member of the War Department hardly encourages such a hope. Said he, in effect: In a few more years there will be only ten or a dozen colleges operating in this country and they will be military schools where Chaucer and Plato will not be taught! That is perhaps the unauthorized bombast of a typical brass hat, but even if his extravagance be diluted with a plentiful amount of decent academic common sense, it still leaves us with the anxious thought that our opportunity to teach religion— as a subject culturally important if nothing else—in a liberal educational program will hardly be augmented by the present tendency. If Chaucer is out for the duration, where, one may ask, will Christ be?

Freedom of religion: the bondage that holds it is, in all candor—and we should add contrition—our cynicism, our pride, our lack of moral and intellectual courage, ethical thoroughness and passion. These are our shackles, and with religion in bondage, irreligion enjoys a field day. Note the attitude expressed in the quotation from a distinguished editorial page:

It would be a grievous error if we were to be so squeamish as to allow questions of ethics to prevent the employment of any weapon that would help us win the war.

Extended comment might be made on many of the phrases in that one sentence. Suffice it to say that it represents something of the current ethical nihilism resulting from the exigency of war. What is more ominous than the way we have personally clapped handcuffs on our normal moral repugnance to the political chicanery that the reports of the North African campaign have turned up? Bribery was "necessary" to "save lives." Grant it, if one must. But to boast of it as if it were a new access of virtue, a new level of rectitude, is to talk the language of those who are slaves to necessity and who find their bondage tolerable by calling it freedom. Is this what is happening to man's ethical sensitivities? Does he not do it to himself? No alien despot could make him *think* his way to the point where chicanery becomes chivalry! It has its rebuke in some wise words that appeared in a syndicated essay in the same paper:

No one doubts that the good warrior has the right to deceive his enemies. But what is inadmissable in the war we are fighting is that we should deceive ourselves—that we should make a virtue of necessity and boast of our guile and turn the moral world upside down by insisting wrong is right and bad is good.

That is a sin, and we have been guilty of it and of this sin we must purge ourselves, or it will corrupt us and corrode our causes and bring us to a black despair of which . . . anxiety . . . is only the first preliminary foreboding.[3]

[5]

It is not pleasant to find ourselves, in a land that speaks proudly of the freedom it concedes to every man to worship as he pleases, or not at all if he wants it that way, spiritually in bondage to the twin subtleties, Social and Intellectual Respectability. It has left us a prey to those who, under the pretense of spurious spiritual aims have exploited us for political, social or economic inter-

[3] Walter Lippmann, December 24, 1942. Copyright, New York *Tribune* Inc.

ests. And we are even proud of it, raising hands heavy
with shackles and calling them garlands. Where such
spiritual debility has not overcome the bearers of the
Christian tradition, where, that is, religion has remained
free, it has stood as the most powerful barricade against
tyranny. In Germany, indeed, it has been the only
openly organized adversary.

Freedom of religion is being lost here, not primarily
through the machinations of an angry alien who would
take it from us in order to put a newly revived ancient
paganism in its place, not by our government in Washington, the state capitol or the city hall. Rather by our
own neglect of spiritual disciplines and the consequent
easy denial of ethical restraints on our lives. This latter
consequence is well-nigh unavoidable. The ratio of
ethical guidance to philosophical reflection in religion
is the same that action bears to thought everywhere.
Ethics is by all odds the most important part of the
religious testimony. If religion is fettered, its ethical
emphasis is lost, and the result is moral chaos. What
then are we to do when, having achieved political freedom for Europe and Asia and Africa, we discover that
prior to or during the process we have lost our religion?

The President has done us an important service in
bringing the need for free religion to our attention.
Not the least significant result of this has been to discover the enemies of religion in our midst. This brings

us to the last question with which this chapter began: How shall religion be set free among us? Writing concerning the Toulon episode, Lippmann said: "Freedom is something which no people can have except from itself." This is as true of religious freedom as of political freedom. How shall it be won for us?

Not by coercion, either by arms or laws, but only by a personal return to wholesome religious inquiry and spiritual discipline. This is harder than paying taxes or waging global war since it is accomplished voluntarily or not at all. And yet the job is ours, if we are to take the President seriously. However formidable it may appear, it is not impossible. Our country was cradled in religion that had both intellectual and social respectability and moral fecundity. No reading of history can miss that central and determinative fact. How was such a situation maintained against the assaults of those who did not believe in freedom of religion?

We suggest four ways. First: there was a Constitutional bulwark. Strong as this was, it was perhaps the least important since it provided only a framework within which free religion was to range. Second: a common belief that the Christian church was a fellowship which both preserved and shared the vital elements of religious experience. Third: a confidence in the practical effectiveness of spiritual disciplines and moral restraints on behavior. Fourth: a participation in direct social action that gave expression to the moral urgency of one's quest for God.

Times have changed, to be sure, but it is hardly to be argued that our present context has made any of these four principles less indispensable than they were three hundred years ago. On the contrary. And if this be so, and if we are to recover the sense of religious freedom that then made incredible suffering worth enduring we can do so in no other way than by invoking afresh these four dynamic religious expedients.

Free religion has nothing to fear save an indolent and proud spirit. There is no peril in humanism; humanism is not the opposite of theism but its complement. The antithesis of humanism is animalism, and it is the latter that is regarded—rightly or otherwise—as a soulless existence. There is a reversion to animalism in the world. It manifests itself in the ferocity of some men and in the apathy of others. If, for the moment there is no anger directed against religion among us, let us be all the more vigilant to detect the apathy that is always close by the spirit of each of us. Our salvation comes by returning to four great American principles, or still further back to the Epistle of St. Paul to the Ephesians, or still further back to him who gave enduring and redemptive meaning to freedom as he preached his first sermon in Nazareth.[4]

[4] Luke 4:14-20.

For those who have traced those three stages of the long trek from bondage to freedom there need be no fear that the roadway to the presence of the Eternal will be barricaded, or that the hands they lift in devotion to God or lower in service to their fellows will be manacled. If they are seeking religious freedom for themselves and for everybody everywhere, let them be encouraged by an ancient and irrevocable promise:

Upon this rock I will build my church and the gates of hell shall not prevail against it.[5]

[5] Matt. 16:18.

The Lord is my shepherd; I shall not want.
Ps. 23:1
And his disciples say unto him, whence should we have so much bread in the wilderness, as to fill so great a multitude?
MATT. 15:33

> Some have too much, yet still do crave;
>   I little have, and seek no more:
> They are but poor, though much they have,
>   And I am rich with little store:
> They poor, I rich; they beg, I give;
> They lack, I have; they pine, I live.
EDWARD DYER, 1540-1607

3

FREEDOM FROM WANT

. . . dismissed the Atlantic Charter as representing aims which were either already an integral part of the American system . . . freedom of speech and worship . . . or were practicably unattainable . . . freedom from want and fear.[1]

The point of our whole presentation has been that the Four Freedoms are only to be understood fully by those who see in them great spiritual aims; and that they will not be achieved if their spiritual implications are lost in the political struggles that are certain to revolve

---

[1] From an address by a well-known economist as reported in the Cleveland *Plain Dealer*.

about them. Hence we have argued that freedom of speech is valid because of the moral element that gives uniqueness to this method of human communication, and that it is safe only when those who are spiritually sensitive to this fact exercise the discipline that alone can adequately control one's utterances. Similarly in the case of the freedom of religion. No argument needs to be made for the spiritual quality that authenticates true religion, yet we need to confront the fact that the restraints put upon the practice of religion are more likely to be those we lay upon our spirits than those that an alien tyranny threatens. If we are to be the exporters and evangelists of free speech and free religion, we must have stock piles ready lest when the days of rebuilding the world are at hand we find that we have too little of the spirit or the commodity for ourselves, much less for global consumption.

[1]

The quotation at the head of this chapter is an indication of what takes place in an otherwise enlightened mind when the problem of freeing the world from want and fear is raised. To say that freedom of speech and worship are an integral part of the American system is true only if the American system is considered from the point of view of politics. To say, furthermore, that freedom from want and fear are practically unattainable is true only if they are to be sought by political expedients. Sensitive to the despair which inspires such predictions the O.W.I. says:

Freedom from want is neither a conjurer's trick nor a madman's dream. The earth has never known it, nor anything approaching it. But free men do not accept the defeatist notion that it never will.[2]

Here is set forth in clear implication the difference between the two approaches to the matter. "The earth has never known it"; that is the hard fact the economist sees; "free men do not accept the . . . notion that it never will" is the spiritual fact that the true realist sees. That such spiritual realism is not the vestige of a now obsolete piety or simple churchmindedness is apparent from another quotation from a familiar column:

The fear is groundless that the promotion of prosperity in the outer world will diminish it in our own. It will enhance it . . . if only we do not suffer the catastrophe . . . of a post war administration composed of men who do not understand the dynamics of the modern social order. Since 1920 men have discovered the principle of prosperity. This discovery is the most important advance in human knowledge in modern times.[3]

Mr. Lippmann would be the first to explain "the dynamics of the modern social order" as something spiritually sustained and ethically motivated.

[2] "Four Freedoms," Washington, D. C., Office of War Information.

[3] Walter Lippmann. Copyright, New York *Tribune* Inc.

[2]

We are confronted then with the President's proposal that men the world around, as a possible long-range result of the victory of the United Nations, shall be freed from want. Freedom of speech is the basis of democracy and since democracy is a matter of man's relation to his fellows in government, his speech must be kept free. Religion is a matter of man's relation to the ideal good in worship and service and must therefore be kept free. Freedom from want, at first glance, deals with man's relation to his material goods. This represents his economic need. During the last one hundred and fifty years this has grown from a purely physical necessity to a criterion of judgment of all values and all types of power. Hence, a culture that boasts both a high level of material, aesthetic and intellectual value, and a high potential of physical energy naturally asserts that man must be free economically. That freedom from want is being perverted by some to mean free enterprise should occasion no surprise. On the contrary it may well serve as a warning.

Some years ago a Chinese proverb, encountered in the course of an effort to read a Chinese novel, yielded this translation:

The starving man makes no complaint though coarse should be his fare;

The freezing man is grateful for the poorest rags to wear;
He seldom stops to choose a road who's fleeing for his life;
The pauper's not particular of whom he takes to wife.

These four unhappy men represent a universal preoccupation which, in the minds of some, makes concern with freedom of speech and the freedom of religion irrelevant. The starving, the freezing, the fugitive, the disinherited—their disabilities are the pressing problems of our day. For this reason we discover that our concern that want be abolished finds fanatical support in the leader of Europe's promised New Order. He is unimpressed by man's need of free religion or unbridled speech, but he has promised one thousand years of freedom from want and fear, and so urgent has been the need that his people have followed him in an effort to win it with impossible weapons at staggering and insupportable cost.

But we are not sure that the problem is as simple as taking care of the four hapless Chinese in the proverb. If that were all there is to it, we could leave it to the economists and get along with other matters. Stuart Chase has written in his gay and plausible manner of the simple way in which we in America can be rid forever of the bogey of food, shelter and clothing scarcity. He supports his encouraging predictions with reams of figures as prim as they are precise.

We accept that hopeful prospect for America without dissent. But in another article in *Harper's*, great doubt is cast upon any such roseate dawn for those who have been living in the darkness of Europe's bitter privations. Hiram Motherwell[4] draws up a balance sheet of "Europe after the Second World War with the regrettable certainty that it can err only on the side of being too conservative." These are what we who promise freedom from want to everybody everywhere in the world will face when the war is done: no food, wealth destroyed, land depleted, machines and equipment deteriorated, lack of consumer's goods, devastation of human life, confusion over property and land titles, demoralization of finance, non-existent currency, unemployed labor, conflicting social classes, and hate. It is a catalogue of horrors indeed. Do we share the President's enthusiasm for the job once we have been confronted by its magnitude?

The concluding paragraph of Motherwell's disquieting essay, however, strikes an unexpected note. Capping the list of Europe's post-war disabilities, in his judgment, is "the volume of hate (that) will be released on Armistice Day." This, he wisely observes will make doubly difficult the rehabilitation contemplated in the devastation analyzed above. Now hate is an attitude of the human spirit and it is this spiritual sickness that

[4] Hunger, Hatred, and Postwar Europe—*Harper's* Magazine, December, 1942.

will make economic recovery immeasurably difficult. "Let us hope" says the author, "that it can be turned somehow against brute nature, so that in the frenzy of reconstruction . . . Europe may at last purge its tortured soul. Yet it seems to me that this will be the peculiar mission of the churches. Surely never before has it been more necessary for the salvation of man here below that divine authority should proclaim in words of steel: 'vengeance is *mine; I* will repay, saith the Lord'."

It is frankly surprising and not a little gratifying that a discussion of the freeing of Europe from economic want can be summarized in such terms. "Tortured soul"—exactly; "necessary for the salvation of man here below"—indeed; "divine authority"—nothing less. Whatever else such an emphasis may be thought to do, it gives us what we think is the proper perspective for our study of freedom from want.

[3]

It is good that we clarify our language at the start. What is it the President means when he speaks of want? Our colloquial use of the word is harmlessly misleading; it signifies desire and lists as equivalents the cognate words, crave, yearn, wish, long for, etc. But surely this was not what Mr. Roosevelt meant. It would be a weird world that never wanted anything: no longing, no family; no wishing, no invention; no desire, no companionship or society; no yearning, no worship; no hunger of soul, no sense of God. The death of desire is the death of everything. To be free from want thus understood is to be free to die.

The correct meaning of the word—and its contrast with our colloquial use—was made clear one day when an exasperated parent was heard to say that what an ill-natured child "wanted" was a sound thrashing. American ears gave instant attention; the speaker was an Englishman. He was not saying that the child yearned, craved, wished or longed for the sort of attention he needed; he was saying there was a deficit, a lack, a scarcity in the child's proper castigatory quota which, both in the interests of abstract justice and practical harmony should be immediately supplied. This is what the third freedom proposes; to be free from want is not to be free from the desire which is the spur of all conscious action; it is rather to be free from the deficit which is often the deterrent to action. Before we can begin to live, we must have had adequate prenatal nourishment; and as we live we must be free from illness, hunger, loneliness, exposure, etc. It is most likely that the four unhappy men of our proverb would listen to exhortations about free speech and free religion if they were concurrently assured that all their deficits in the matters of eating, dressing, resting and wiving would be normally made up.

These four obligations are very real and no one claiming interest in the spiritual focus of our inquiry has a right to neglect the hard facts of material deficits. The church is culpable at that point, and its neglect has furnished the basis for the criticism of the anti-pie-in-the-sky crowd. Whenever the concern of the church for the spirits of men blinds her to her obligations to aid men in securing their essential physical needs, she is false to her charter. No one can charge her Founder with such an error. In fact there are points where it is difficult and inadvisable to separate the spiritual from the physical want. For this reason a brief survey of the economic aspect may serve as preliminary to the more specific emphasis of these studies.

[4]

The problem envisioned in the third freedom is: how to make both ends meet? Many are working on this in terms of adequate wage scales. The University of California prepared recently a wartime budget for a family of four based on San Francisco prices as of March, 1942. The budget is described by the Labor Research Association as the most satisfactory one yet prepared by an academic or governmental agency. It calls for $49.63 a week, or $2,580.82 a year. Food takes

32.4 per cent of the total—and food prices have advanced since the budget was prepared; main savings come out of items for clothing, house furnishings and the like; expenditures for recreation, gifts, etc. are cut down in order that the average American family may pay war taxes and buy war bonds. With war taxes and bonds still to come out of their $2,580.82 a year, the University of California budget family would have exactly one tenth as much to live on as a wealthy family which was restricted to the $25,000 wartime top income.[5]

To supply the necessities of a wartime budget for all of the people of the United States calls for the most exact scientific calculation and planning. It is shocking to realize that such a program is becoming increasingly the object of political dispute and threatens to be crucial in the postwar struggle for power. That certain interests cry out against the ideal of "a quart of milk for every Hottentot" is less a reflection of indifference to economic deficits in the African jungles than unconcern over the bondage of impoverishment under which American slum dwellers live. This arraigns the intelligence of the protesters, but it more seriously indicts their souls. They fail to understand the nature of the human spirit, and such failure has been articulate in the two extremes of nonscientific ministering to want. The first

[5] From *In Fact*, edited by George Seldes.

says the way to satisfy mankind is to reduce his desires to the vanishing point. If you want nothing, you are satisfied with everything! This is complete nihilism in politics, personality, development and morals. The result is a starvation diet for a while and a Buddhist nirvana shortly afterward forever.

Hardly less extreme, though more alluring is the idea that man will be satisfied if the supply for his needs can be raised to the surplus level. If you have everything, you want nothing! Thus has Western Christendom swung to the opposite pole from Eastern Buddhism. But, as has been said, each of these extremes has lost sight of the nature of the human spirit. The first dwarfs all growth by crippling the primary human impulse—the desire to live fully. The second assumes that the gratification of all physical desire is the measure of the full life. The first ends in death; the second ends in surfeit, and surfeit is spiritual death. Socrates, so it is said, upon entering a market in Athens looked about him and describing a pair of circles with a sweeping, impatient gesture, cried: "Ye gods, that there should be so many things that Socrates doesn't want." That was twenty-five hundred years ago. It has its parallel in a more recent news item. Of Edna May Oliver, late screen favorite, the following comment was made on the occasion of her death:

For 30 years she lived out of a trunk. She climbed to small bedrooms in hotels all over the world and dreamed of a home of her own. Ten years ago she came to Hollywood and for three years saved almost her whole salary. Then she bought one of those movie houses, super de luxe, with a 40 foot living room and an air conditioner in the attic. As she told this writer last summer: "I've never felt at home in it. I've been like an old fire horse at range. There's too much room in that house. And too many possessions. And too much worry about whether the roses will get mildewed. I'm going home. I'm selling the house and I'm going to rent me a room and be happy.

Miss Oliver was a great comedienne, but she was not trying to be funny in that interview. The last two words are the key to freedom from want: "Be happy." We shall return to this later.

There is a way to make ends meet and it begins by recognizing the legitimacy of our needs. The advertisers exploit this masterfully. If we took our cue from billboard and radio as to what our needs are, we would be breathless from morning to night rushing "right now or at the latest tomorrow" to grocer or druggist in pursuit of deodorants or cold tablets. We do not, however, fall into such hands if for no other reason than the complexity of such advice. We have ways of knowing what our needs are without depending either on our somewhat unpredictable impulses or radio programs. And oddly enough, an advertisement in *Time* of November 6, 1942, under the trademark of Pan American Air-

ways puts the matter very clearly. What are our needs?
Herewith the statement:

(1) Every child should find itself a member of a family
housed with decency and dignity, so that it may grow
up in a happy fellowship unspoiled by underfeeding—
or over crowding, by dirty and drab surroundings or
by mechanical monotony of environment.

(2) Every child should have the opportunity of an education till years of maturity. This education should be
inspired by faith in God and find its focus in worship.

(3) Every citizen should be secure in possession of such
income as will enable him to maintain a home and
bring up children in such conditions as are described
in paragraph 1 above.

(4) Every citizen should have a voice in the conduct of
the business or industry which is carried on by means
of his labor, and the satisfaction of knowing that his
labor is directed to the well-being of the community.

(5) After the war, every citizen should have sufficient
daily leisure, with two days of rest in seven, and an
annual holiday with pay, to enable him to enjoy a full
personal life.

(6) Every citizen should have assured liberty in the forms
of freedom of worship, of speech, of assembly, and of
association for special purposes.

These are basal needs and can be simplified thus: every
individual in the world needs: a family properly housed,
an education properly conducted, an income properly
secured, a voice in government and business properly
protected, a measure of leisure properly organized, and
freedom of worship and assembly properly maintained.
If these are basal wants then it is possible to measure

accurately our basal deficits. Not in terms of two
chickens in every pot or two cars in every garage (how
remote that seems today!), but in terms of the things
that make a full life possible. If need and deficit are
both known, to fail to organize the world in terms
wiping out all deficits must be laid to spiritual obtuseness or moral apathy. This is the freedom from want
we are proposing to guarantee to the world.

[5]

This takes in much too much territory; two of the
freedoms already discussed are included as basal needs
in the above list. It shapes up more nearly like an ideal
world, not merely a world assured of four freedoms.
And yet there is one significant need left out; it is the
need or deficit which must be supplied if all the others
are not to fail utterly. It is the will-to-share.

Many have already recognized the Pan American Air-
ways advertisement as a statement made by the genial
and workmanlike Archbishop of Canterbury covering
his vision for a postwar world. He was too wise a man,
however, to end his summary with paragraph six. It is
necessary, as we have said, to know accurately what the
rudimentary human needs are in the modern world before we can plan to supply them. But why is it that
these needs, measurably known hitherto have not been
met in anything like a measurable proportion? Is it not

because of the fatal lack of the moral and spiritual impulse to act for human relief in terms of human demands instead of human caprice?

The Archbishop is not quite so explicit, but he has not missed the point; for immediately under the six paragraphs quoted there occurred in the ad this interesting addendum:

I should give a false impression of my own convictions if I did not here add that there is no hope of establishing a more Christian social order except through the labor and sacrifice of those in whom the spirit of Christ is active.

He has been careful to add that the primary requisite for everything the race of man needs—a condition which he describes as "a more Christian social order" is "the labor and sacrifice of those in whom the spirit of Christ is active."

One needs no better statement of the spiritual basis for freedom from want than this provides, and yet these words, far from settling our problem, create or point up another. Basal to a settlement of all needs is the labor and sacrifice of those in whom the spirit of Christ is active. The question arises: Is there any lack of such a spirit?

[6]

This takes us back again to the proposition that man's primary needs are spiritual. Testimony supporting this is abundant among the ancients. What of the realization of this among moderns? From strange places and stranger circumstances comes the intimation of an answer.

The Russians are finding that old values and spiritual forces which have moved men for thousands of years have their roots in the eternal nature of humanity.

Thus wrote one who, knowing Russia intimately, reflected upon the significance of the recent appointment of a high church dignitary to an important post in the Soviet Union. It was not very long ago, we recall, that the government was thought to have purged the nonsense about spiritual forces from the mind of Mother Russia.

Immediately following the first reports of the spectacular successes of General Alexander's Eighth Army in Africa the Associated Press wired this somewhat unusual comment:

The picked men of the German Africa Corps remain brave and defiant as long as they are fighting but wilt once they surrender.

Some give way to tears and others chatter nervously about the terrific bombings they have taken for weeks. Most of them seem devout, some wearing crosses about their necks, and others carrying Bibles.

Such quotations as these prove nothing in general; in particular they only support the notion that nothing can ultimately destroy the spiritual sensitivity of men. But to believe that is to accept a good deal. For if what is primarily necessary in achieving freedom from want is a spiritual quality, it is good to know first that such quality is a fundamental component of the human individual, and second that no agony or terror can wholly destroy it.

On the other hand, it is likely that mere well-being itself may corrode the will-to-share. No clearer evidence of the lack of the "sacrifice of those in whom the spirit of Christ is active" is needed than a comment from a widely syndicated column concerning the Vice-President whose utterances of late seem to indicate that he has taken the Four Freedoms seriously:

Wallace is a lover of humanity but somehow he never seems able to get the same love out of humanity that he gives. He talked as if Russia and the United States would have the same ideals and the same kind of democracies after the war. But he had to give a new definition of democracy. He implied any government devoted to the common man was democracy, although sometimes it had to be run by one man. If that is the definition, it is not our kind of democracy but dictatorship, in one of its fascist, communal or socialist forms.

In other words, Henry Wallace, who because he loves humanity and wants to see the freedom from want accomplished, is either a fascist or communist or socialist dictator!

[7]

It is important for us to think of the tragic deficits in the supply of man's necessary physical goods. They are staggering enough, and each day adds to the terrible aggregate. When we get around to it, the physical job will be beyond all possible present calculations. Before that, however, there is the demand for the discovery of new deposits of spiritual energy, inclination, and hardihood without which the enterprise will not even be undertaken.

We will do well to face up to this—to the lack, that is, of inclination, the lack of the will-to-sacrifice and labor under the impetus of the spirit of Christ. The struggle between the idealist (so condemned) and the realist (so-called) that will follow the end of the military struggle is already taking shape. It is no oversimplification of the conflict to state it in spiritual terms, for those who will go all-out for the liberation of the hungry from their terrible prison will be animated by one moral ideal, and those who will oppose such romantic dreaming will be impelled by quite another. And the difference between them lies in the quality of spirit that characterizes each. When the fatigue and disillusionment that is the shoddy harvest of every war is gathered into the victor's barns, the sound of the three words—freedom from want—will mean only one thing to one side—"back to the good old days"; and any serious proposal to become Europe's Santa Claus will make the three words odious.

It takes no prescience to predict this; it is openly avowed by important spokesmen. Westbrook Pegler's column is called "Fair Enough." One might discuss at some length the somewhat sinister meanings hidden in that urbane title. If it were representative only of Mr. Pegler's acidulous ideas of fairness it would be one thing; but that it is representative of the attitude of certain powerful American interests is quite another matter. A good deal of notice has been taken of his strictures against the New Deal, and his anti-Roosevelt exhortations have been properly rebuked elsewhere. But he is now the advocate of official isolationism, the sort of selfish blindness that followed World War I and set up the pins for the World War II ball to knock down in the next alley. In his column of December 30, 1942, commenting characteristically on Mr. Henry Wallace's speech about the need for the reeducation of Europeans and Japanese after the war he said:

The alternative would seem to be for the United States to withdraw in isolation and armed preparedness to wait out the future and reclaim the liberties which have been narrowed by the war emergency and re-establish their right to work freely, to select their occupations and associates, to own property and engage in trade.

Passing over much that these words evoke, let it be said simply that such a sentiment is as remote from the ideal contained in freedom from want as Pegler is from paradise! He is no doubt honest in his judgment; so also are those whose words he speaks. Their honesty does not ease the tension, however, it increases it. The coming struggle, therefore, between those who are actuated by one spirit and those who are actuated by its opposite will have all the bitterness and finality that characterize honest antagonists. Only those who believe in their cause fight fiercely and to the end. That is why the democratic-fascist struggle in America is—unless all signs fail—going to follow close upon the cessation of war, and continue until one side overwhelms the other. It is the deep conviction of these studies that those whose labor and sacrifice is activated by the spirit of Christ are certain to be on the side of the third freedom and against the neo-isolationism that is in the making on the other side.

Suppose, however, that the people of this abounding land should, by a new access of self-sacrifice, rise to meet the challenge of physical deficit in the world by a surplus spiritual power. It is pleasant to think about ships laden with the stores from our ever-normal granary, which by our voluntary privations we have made available for Europe and Asia's hungry, plying the waters of the sea on errands of mercy. Would that be the final guarantee against the bondage of want to which we have been pledged? No, not unless man does live by bread and shelter alone. And that is essentially what this war is about—what the Four Freedoms are set forth to prove to a world that has felt so strongly that bread and circuses, rubber and tin, Blut and Boden were the be-all and end-all of life that they have attacked the world in order to get them. In other words again, back beyond and deep beneath the whole concept of freedom from want lies the primary spiritual problem of the ultimate nature of man's spirit. What is it he wants, the failure to satisfy which will drive him to the madness of violence?

Whatever else is to be said about the relation of the Christian tradition to the pattern of Western culture, it is obvious that the spiritual struggle stirring beneath the issues involved in freeing the world from want has been going on for nineteen centuries. Ever since the profound insight concerning the inadequacy of physical possessions for the satisfaction of man's basic needs stirred the great prophetic spirits to utterance, it has created conflict. The conflict between class and class, nation and nation, race and race have their counterpart in the tension within the individual over the question of which quest shall be the dominant: Mammon or God; the things of the spirit or the flocks and harvests of the fields. And nearly always Mammon has raised the pennon of victory over the disheveled and prostrate spirit of embattled humanity.

But all the while man has secretly resisted the conqueror, though he has often made him a friend, hoping thus to subjugate him ultimately. Those who have tried to persuade mankind that his life does consist in the abundance of the things he possesses have had their open followers; and those who have said man's deep and satisfying rewards come from the things of the spirit have had their secret partisans. Now the conflict has dilated from the small circle of a personal decision to the vast circumference of a world fighting for things. And yet it is a symptom of the eternal wistfulness of the spirit that while we kill and destroy and reassert our claims on the lands of earth, we still talk fondly about freedom of speech and of religion, of freedom from want and fear.

This is what makes crucial our effort to understand and realize these aims—these four freedoms. Some have said that we have this chance as our last. Lose this and the door is shut. This is why, still further, we must understand the deficits we are to supply, not alone in terms of consumer's goods. In America we have not yet come to any unanimous faith in the primacy of spiritual well-being. We have not yet resolved the dilemma which disquiets us no end; namely, that our efforts to establish a condition of sufficiency of material goods often leaves us spiritually unhealthy; that a comfort-focused civilization forfeits the spiritual genius that privation and sacrifice produce. Our uneasy consciences will make it simple enough for us to send some ships of surplus foods and machines by which the lid of the dungeon in which Europe is held after the war may be lifted. Better—or worse—we can do our noble uttermost and rehabilitate the devastated world and persuade the revived and happy people that now that they are free from physical deficits their problems are solved. Paradoxically that is the road that leads always to war since the wish for fuller and fuller satisfactions—insatiable as they are—produce the jealousies and the hatreds that ultimately flower into the horrid foliage of destruction. The business of freeing the world from want involves, as an initial step, freeing ourselves from fatal notions about what our wants are. Our materialistic success is the envy of the world; our materialism is its scorn; and unless we are willing to undertake an enterprise that will teach the world the error of our ways as a part of the business of saving the world from the poverty of its food supply, we had better not undertake it. Of course we can do relief work with a sense of pious patronage, but that will be as far from freedom from want in the world as the Salvation Army barracks is from utopia. Little wonder some say, from exasperation or moral cowardice, that "isolation is the only alternative."

[8]

We insist it is no retreat from realism to talk of life's ultimate values as basically spiritual. The obituary of the opposite view has been written by one who has no religious ax to sharpen. Peter Drucker on page 268 of his book *The End of Economic Man* says—and it is the last sentence in the book:

The new society must be accomplished by forces of a far more basic nature [more basic than economic]. . . . The next decade will decide whether Europe can find such forces which will lead her out of the impasse into which the collapse of Economic Man has maneuvered her, through the darkness of totalitarian fascism before she finds a new, positive, noneconomic concept of free and equal man.[6]

What he said of Europe in 1939 is becoming dangerously true of America in 1943 with this as yet significant difference: because of the exemptions we have enjoyed —our relative freedom from want and fear, of religion and speech—we have been allowed to keep alive ideally a "noneconomic concept of free and equal man." It is not new, nor will the groping of Europe discover a new concept. It is as old as the ethical and spiritual component of our culture. However, it may have been scorned or forgotten, it is still a beacon of hope to both

[6] Peter Drucker: *The End of Economic Man*, New York: The John Day Company, 1939.

man and society. It says, and it has proved true times
without number, that a man's life or the life of a nation
does not consist of the abundance of things it possesses.
Any attempt to secure freedom from want in disregard
of that primary moral and spiritual fact moves forward
with the saboteur of its ultimate success in its own ranks.

[9]

No small part of the problem of achieving freedom
from want is preventing the liberation of materialistic
greed in the process. And the guarantee against such a
calamity is not in the hands of politically motivated
men. The Archbishop's phrase: "the labor and sacrifice
of those in whom the spirit of Christ is active" suggests
the polar antithesis of the opportunistic use of any
available expedient employed in the struggle for power.
And this means, simply, that the full realization of freedom number three can come only through the impulses
that have been the dynamics of the Christian tradition.
If the world is to be saved from spiritual deficit—which
must be made up before freedom from material wants
can be attained and made safe—it is the job of those
who, as we have so often said, possess and cherish the
spiritual insights of our religion. It is not to be expected
that those whose understanding of material possessions
is pagan will, when the going gets tough, go all out for
number three all over the world. Those who see the

relation of goods to man's spiritual satisfactions will stay with such a global obligation so long as their reserves are not exhausted.

To put a considerable part of this program upon the Christian fellowship as we have felt it necessary to do with regard to freedom of religion and speech, is to take nothing away from others who share a concern for it. It is rather to say that here, as always, the Christian fellowship confronts again its eternal and irreversible commission. Secularists are saying that unless spiritual deficits are repaired the material rehabilitation of the world may be the prelude to another ghastly effort at global suicide. If we say it is our job, we say it not arrogantly but with a humility that is not cant because it is contrite.

This involves personal discipline of the most assiduous sort, a discipline to be begun by taking inventory. How adequate is my resource of labor and sacrifice? How much of my behavior is activated by the spirit of Christ? Until I am sure of my answers here, I cannot ask the church to bend its energies to so prodigious a task. Much less shall I be willing to trust it to those who know nothing of the meaning of spiritual poverty.

[10]

"Freedom from want," says the O.W.I. brochure, "is within the grasp of man. . . . The beginning has been made. The right to work. The right to fair pay. The right to adequate food, clothing, shelter, medical care. . . . It is a people's own experiment and goes on through the courtesy of chemists and physicists and poets and technicians and men of strong faith and unshakable resolve."

We would add: "the right to spiritual replenishment" to the three mentioned, and underline the words "men of strong faith and unshakable resolve," for they are the spiritually vital, the undiscourageables. It is they to whom One greater than Canterbury gave a mandate that was a key to the lock that had shut off spiritually destitute men from the source of strong faith and unshakable resolve in his day. It goes:

Seek ye first the Kingdom of God [free religion], and his righteousness [free speech], and all these things shall be added unto you [freedom from want].[7]

To win that for everybody everywhere in the world is a big order; but it is the key that will open dungeons, and the hammer that will strike the manacles from the wrists of the manifold bondsmen of the world.

[7] Matt. 6:33.

Yea, though I walk through the valley of the shadow of death, I will fear no evil, for thou art with me.   Ps. 23:4

Say ye not, A Confederacy . . . neither fear ye their fear, nor be afraid.   Isa. 8:12

True nobility is exempt from fear.
SHAKESPEARE: *Henry VI*, PART II, ACT IV

In masks outrageous and austere
The years go by in single file;
But none has merited my fear
And none has quite escaped my smile.
ELINOR HOYT WYLIE:
Let No Charitable Hope

4

FREEDOM FROM FEAR

PART I

" 'Fear' *writes Professor Ferrero, 'is the soul of the living universe.' Animals and men are animated by the urge to avoid danger. 'But man is not only afraid of real and imaginary danger; he is frightened of his own power to frighten others.' This is why, in an organized society, the primary function of government is to protect people against 'the two greatest fears of mankind—anarchy and war.'* "
"*The only thing we have to fear is fear itself.*" [1]

Fear is a state of mind or, to keep strictly within the circumference of these studies, fear is a spiritual condi-

[1] President Franklin Delano Roosevelt, first inaugural address, March 4, 1933.

tion. This is what has been set forth as the substantial fact about speech, religion and want. The essence of speech is spiritual in that it is the highest medium of human communication and because the employment of language is implicitly a moral act. Therefore freedom of speech can be understood only spiritually and secured ultimately through inner compulsions. Freedom of speech as a political expedient lies on a level far beneath that upon which the essence of speech properly operates. Religion manifestly is a spiritual exercise and by its nature can escape the mesh of any net that seeks to prison it. This is not to claim exemptions; it is to warn that the real encroachments on the freedom of the religious enterprise are those we allow or fashion ourselves, those shackles of pride, insensitivity or moral indolence which already operate among us to discourage and retard the progress of man's spirit toward the Divine. Similarly, but with less obviousness, want rests on spiritual emplacements. The material needs of humankind are not uniform because the spiritual dispositions of men are different. To satisfy some is to surfeit others, to starve the body of one may, oddly enough, feed his soul. Only spiritual understanding of man's basal wants will provide against the extravagant generosity of some whose very charity might impoverish others. If man's needs are only for food and shelter, there is little hope that he will cease the effort to secure them by violent assault on those who have them. Such an understanding of the three freedoms already discussed does not remove them from reality even though it shifts the emphasis of inquiry from one factor of life to another. The very fact that the President's war aims are presented as four components of a great whole called Freedom, and the further fact that freedom is always a spiritual experience, primarily and ultimately beyond the reach of political expedients—which, confessedly may be indirectly an aid in winning it—these support the contention that the Four Freedoms confront us with a great spiritual challenge, which, if it be allowed to fall to the level of merely crying a slogan, will render all our blood, sweat, toil and tears a prodigal and irreparable waste.

[1]

Fear, by consensus, shares with religion a fixed place in the category of the spiritual. Indeed, by being a clearly established state of mind, it is more substantially spiritual—if the contradiction between substance and spirit may be allowed to stand—than religion. For this reason much of religion is to be exactly described as fear. The

. . . one unchanged obsession, wheresoe'er my feet have
        trod
. . . a keen, enormous, haunting, never-sated thirst for God

of Gamaliel Bradford's poem[2] might be a frantic, head-
long, unabated *fear* of God and still be authenticated
as religion.

We have already alluded to the inconsequential order
of the Four Freedoms in the various statements given
us. If they had been presented with a studied regard
for their interrelation and ranking importance, the
chances are that the last would have been first, though
in this case the scriptural precedent would not neces-
sarily have made the first last. Democracy, religion,
economics, psychology—these were set forth at the beginning as the fields within which the freedoms were to
operate, and it takes no argument to support the claim
that all the others are so conditioned by psychological
factors as to determine, almost completely their quality.
As a matter of fact, if we are not to be free of fear we
can have no freedom of any sort. The religion that is
afraid is religion on a very low level; laws conceding
man's right to speak freely are meaningless if, for any
reason, he is afraid to talk. And of what good is it to
promise freedom from want if the act of accepting such
a boon is paralyzed by any one of the terrors that may
surround it?

Our age has been correctly designated as the Great
Age of Fear. No doubt earlier ages were overwhelmed

[2] "God." From *Shadow Verses*, by Gamaliel Bradford, Yale
University Press.

by periodic fears; constant anxiety and dread were the lot of the primitive to whom nature was always a malign and capricious companion. The Greek feared fate with a sedate sort of reverence and accommodated himself to Nemesis with resignation that while sometimes appearing defiant to the point of gaiety was nevertheless grim and cheerless.

But our day leaves little of the dark unfathomed deeps of fear unsounded. We have conquered nature, and now are afraid of our use of it; we are less afraid of our weakness than we are of our power. It has been the rule hitherto to fear one's enemies; but the depth of the abyss that yawns before the world's unsteady feet is seen in the awful fact that in some countries, one fears one's friends. In Germany, we are told, even one's family is not to be trusted.

Global war means global fear, and global fear means world-wide neurosis. Twenty-five years ago Basil King's extensively read book summed up what was then an appalling diagnosis of the virulence of fear in the sick body of the world. To the mind of today it is so mild as to be almost amusing.

Every one is living or working in fear. The mother is afraid for her children. The father is afraid for his business. The clerk is afraid for his job. The worker is afraid of his boss or his competitor. There is hardly a man who is not afraid that some other man will do him a bad turn. There is hardly a woman who is not afraid that things she craves may be denied her or that what she loves may be snatched away. I am ready to guess that all the miseries wrought by sin and sickness put together would not equal those we bring on ourselves by the means we perhaps do least to counteract. We are not sick all the time, but all the time all of us—or practically all of us—are afraid of some one or something.[3]

We forbear to bring this diagnosis up to date. We would almost settle for King's condition and think we had a bargain—we who live under a legitimate fear that civilization is dying. What is this scourge, this pandemic of the world's spirit?

Those whose business is understanding the mind have something to say. Fear, they reassure us, is one of the unregulated primitive responses that sentient creatures make to life. It is variously called reaction, emotion, instinct. Shakespeare, whose insight was as deep as his language was unprofessional called it passion. "Of all base passions, fear is most accursed." The other two primal human reactions are rage and love. The infant is frightened by a noise or by sudden loss of support; he is angered by restraints placed upon his freedom; he is pleased when he is comfortable and well and will gurgle with delight. This is called love—in such a condition he loves everybody with an innate animal attachment. This means that all normal animals have this

[3] Basil King, *The Conquest of Fear*. New York: Doubleday, Doran & Company, Inc. Copyright, 1921.

thing we call fear as an ingredient of their nature. It exclusively serves life in its own way. The illness we call fear—if such it be—is not only pandemic; it is incurable.

But the doctors go on to tell us that there are two reactions called fear that are neither pandemic nor wholesome. Fear, the undisciplined indigenous reaction, is wholesome, but some of its impersonators are not. The fear of dangerous things that is salutary has one imitator in fear of harmless things, which is silly, and another in the fear of things that do not exist, which is psychotic.

Look for a moment at the fear of harmless things. This is easily educated, and if it persists is often little more than an anxiety neurosis. It is likely to be highly imaginative and unstable. Cervantes makes Don Quixote put it thus: "Fear is sharp-sighted and can see things underground and much more in the skies." Such a mood, we now know, manifests a lack of self-confidence and can be relieved by a wise discipline designed to augment one's belief in oneself.

The fear of things that do not exist is of course a mental illness and should be treated as such. To this problem psychiatrists have brought enormous reassurance in modern times, and to them the task of freeing such persons from fear must be committed.

While it is true that many fear reactions are compounded of all three of these manifestations of insecurity, nevertheless the solid core of normal healthy fear is not difficult to isolate. And this must be done if it is to be properly dealt with. We remember that the President says we must achieve freedom from fear; he even goes so far as to intimate that the fear of fear may be eliminated, though that involves more than our study contemplates. If the fourth freedom is to fulfill its role in the drama of each individual life, its true character must be set forth, and it must stick strictly to its own lines.

Common sense in this regard, is wise with the lore of millions of years. We know that without fear, life is impossible. Timid animals, poorly equipped with protective devices, are endowed with acuteness of sense and fleetness of foot. Thus their survival is possible. In human beings, fear is the teacher of caution, and the fashioner of skill. The motorist, the pilot, the surgeon— these all would dare nothing if they dared all. Fearlessness makes for rashness and danger where fear makes for caution and safety.

The job we have is hardly that of getting rid of fear but of making proper use of it. It is a delicate and powerful mechanism and must be kept in a regulated equilibrium. Tip it too far and it throws all life off balance. Fear that is unconsciously suppressed may return to plague us with a complex; fear that is consciously put aside may find its place occupied by recklessness. To over-encourage fear, on the other hand, is to **invite** feebleness of spirit. The too timid animal starves; the too cautious surgeon would never operate.

If we know that much we fear is illusory, the first job for normal persons—and our discussion from this point on deals only with normal fear—is to understand what he is actually afraid of. It is reported of Robert Browning that he once said there was only one line in English poetry that he coveted as his own. It was written by his friend Arthur Hugh Clough and read: "If hopes be dupes, fears may be liars." Well might Browning have envied the complete sententious wisdom of those words. Our reaction to Clough's line, however, is not envy but gratitude. One of the most salubrious things that can happen to a man is to stop short with a realization that much that he had feared deserved no such gravity, that many of his fears were either pranksters or perjurers. The remark has been variously credited but in this context we allow Henry Ward Beecher's claim to it: "I have seen a great deal of trouble in my life but most of it never happened."

We must not only be sure of certain general considerations in our study of fear. It is important to know what the President was thinking about when he proposed freedom from fear for everybody in the world. Undoubtedly he was speaking from the perspective of statecraft. Our point of view in these discussions has not dealt with the political phases of freedom for we

believe freedom is to be understood in spiritual terms
and won ultimately by spiritual energies. There is a
psychological obligation connected with freedom from
fear. It may be stated thus: To educate fear into prudence and to vitalize prudence into power. Thus one
is freed from fear. There is also a more specifically
spiritual or ethical problem involved. It may be stated
in the language of a familiar verse from the first letter
of Elder John: "There is no fear in love, for perfect love
casteth out fear." We shall have more to say later about
both these phases of the problem. In the meantime,
however, there are certain points with reference to the
statesman's angle that may profitably engage us since it
is within the framework of government that the psychological and spiritual aspects of our problem can be most
dramatically set forth.

[2]

The President wants the world free from fear. Naturally he is concerned that this condition be achieved
in America first. Looking at the job with a concern primarily for our side, we are able to see two things: first,
what it involves in aim and cost; second, what it involves
in methods of dealing with the horrendous.

In the first place the assumption is that the Axis
powers, having numbed with terror the spirits of their
victims and sought by threat and assault to terrorize the

rest of the world not under their savage dominion, must, before anything else is done, be reduced to such utter ruin and powerlessness that neither the fact nor the thought of them will ever stir an eyelash of apprehension among those who formerly feared them. This is the unequivocal mind of those who fight.

Its initial cost—the capital outlay—in human ingenuity and life and in material resources is prodigious beyond our computation. The war is global; the fear is global; and before it is done, the cost may be global. But once the Axis is reduced to impotence, the cost of maintaining such a status will continue to stagger our imaginations and our budgets. Only a powerless adversary is a harmless adversary; only an adversary that can never rise again to threaten is innocuous. Once an enemy is disarmed, steps must be taken to prevent the recrudescence of terror. This, as we are beginning to be told, is going to cost much more than subjugation. How long and how much cannot yet be known. That nothing less than this is contemplated is evidenced by the O.W.I. brochure to which such copious reference has already been made:

The first move to free people from fear is to achieve a peaceable world which has been deprived of its power to destroy itself. This can only be accomplished by disarming the aggressors and keeping them disarmed. Last time they were disarmed, but they were not prevented from rearming. This time they will be disarmed in truth.

We can get a glimpse of the costs of this by opening one door alone. Until men learn to live by disciplining themselves, they will have to be kept orderly by police control. Once the adversary has his arms taken from him, others will have to do his policing for him. Since the job is vastly more than keeping hoodlums in check, extending as it will to the regulation of all life, economic, industrial and even educational, one can see—through the police door—what a costly and intricate undertaking is before us.

Once the argument on the field of battle is settled, and before policing can begin, a general strategy must be agreed upon which will determine the end toward which every expedient is directed. Remember our job will be to set the world free from the fear that is excited by nations on the rampage. Obviously the general strategy that will guide the next step shall not lose sight of the fourth freedom.

Only a powerless nation is a harmless nation. How is this condition to be won? Machiavelli figured that one out a long time ago. He said the only way to treat a conquered nation was either to utterly destroy it—lay waste the land and uproot and destroy the race in stock and branch, or immediately integrate it indissolubly into a new international order. Each of these alternatives has its evangelists today though, oddly enough, both sides would resent being accused of having taken one chance or another in a Machiavellian option.

Perhaps preference in the matter is not so strictly limited as fifteenth century Florentine thought. By the guidance of history we learn there are two ways in which conquered nations have been served. In the light of the present—or of the history that is presently to be made—there is a third. While they are suggested by what has been said about the Machiavellian choice, they are in certain respects significantly different. Let us be reminded again that our choice is to be made with a view to securing freedom from fear, to secure, that is for ourselves and allies once and for all, emancipation from the perennial agony of nationalist wars.

The oldest expedient—it might be called the conventional method of dealing with a conquered foe—has been to reduce him to a state of impotence and then put him to work. In ancient times the foe became a slave, either where he was conquered or in the land of the victor. Antony was proud of this and appealed to it as a defense of his love for Caesar:

> He hath brought many captives home to Rome
> Whose ransoms did the public coffers fill.

That was not ambition, it was smart business. So it has been regarded by Hitler who has performed the Caesarean operation and delivered eight million slaves to the industrial plants of Germany. In 1919 the plan was the same though it worked with other instruments. Germany was made an economic slave, and the terms of the treaty imposed such rigor that the psychology of slavery was as real in Berlin in 1920 as it was in Rome in 44 B.C. The question for us is not whether this is wise from the standpoint of politics or economics, although the answer is not obscure; it is whether it is wise from the standpoint of the fourth freedom. Does one fear a slave less than he fears a foe? The answer is a broad No for the reason that one's slave *is* one's foe. In the autumn of 1919 J. M. Keynes wrote:

There may, therefore be ahead of us a long silent process of semi-starvation, and of a gradual, steady lowering of the standards of life and comfort. The bankruptcy and decay of Europe, if we allow it to proceed, will affect every one in the long run, but perhaps not in a way that is striking or immediate.[4]

That was his protest against reducing Germany to economic serfdom. What he forecast a year after the Armistice is now "striking and immediate." We now know that the fear of Germany's power was not greatly abated even when her armies were demobilized and her navy scuttled. The history of the past twenty years has been the story of a rising tide of fear—the fear the Allies had of the slaves they had created. This is true irre-

[4] *The Economic Consequences of the Peace*, New York: Harcourt, Brace and Company.

spective of considerations of justice; it is true because of the nature of the human spirit. The anger that stirs the heart of the slave—and by such measure as he is spiritually sensitive his anger is ineradicable—that anger is the source of his master's ineradicable fear. If we want fear abolished the way of Caesar and Hitler falls far short of commending itself. To be defended at all, it must be on other grounds.

There is a second way that escaped the imagination of Machiavelli. Indeed it is a product of the world politics he helped create but did not live to see. It sees that the impoverishment of a nation lays heavy penalties on its neighbors, therefore to reduce the enemy to impotence is inexpedient. It is not a question of power versus powerlessness but of a balance of power. Permit him power enough to take care of himself and at the same time to help us frighten others of whom we are afraid. This is a crude way of stating the elegant mythology that has enchanted the rulers of the past one hundred years, but it is not altogether unrealistic. By no means has it yet been abandoned as a possible solution of the current unpleasantness. The fact that Rudolph Hess came to England to propose such a plan has not wholly discredited it. There is no little talk about the wisdom—the necessity indeed—of allowing Germany to regain sufficient strength to stand off the Union of Soviet Socialist Republics which, despite our present affection in arms, inspires in many of us sinister chills of ideological disaffection. Similarly some have felt it good strategy to keep China—our most deserving ally perhaps—strong enough to checkmate Japan but not strong enough to resist Western imperialism. India is put in the same bracket by some.

The method shivers down the spine of our total life. Thus labor is conceded full rights within our national economy in order that it may be kept strong enough to expand production but too weak to change the basic illness that has so long plagued our peacetime economy. So the point might be enlarged to little further advantage. What is important for us is the realization that such balances of power are predicated, not on the elimination of fear, but on its cultivation. It is bad enough to discover, as Keynes did, that to enslave a foe is to perpetuate the enmity that divides him from us and thus keep our fear of him well fueled; it is worse, in all conscience, to deal with our enemies—or our friends—on the basis that if we can be nucleated into the right combinations we can scare off all the other gangs and thus maintain the peace of stalemate.

[3]

These two methods, enslavement and combination-in-restraint-of-power have been the methods used by the human family as it has operated in large groups. Both, we insist, fail to conciliate the demands of the human spirit; in other words they exhibit the sort of spiritual ignorance that is at the bottom of most of our social ineptitude. Furthermore, they are in many respects the opposite of the methods men use as they deal with each other individually. The institution of man-to-man slavery has been discredited as economic folly as well as moral obliquity, and today where men combine in small units of power to threaten each other, they are liable to regulation under the law and indicted by common sense as self-defeating. If we are compelled to choose between them we are doomed first to fear and second to frustration.

It is the shape of the new world that provides us with the contours of a third pattern. If in the centuries that are behind us this has not been tried we may in part lay it to the fact that the disunity of the world has made us overlook it. The emergent world, however, is asking for it with the myriad voices of education, art, religion and business. The singular fact that the combination of warring powers fighting the Axis calls itself the United Nations instead of the Allies points our minds in the new direction. To be allied means to be joined with; to be united means to become a part of, and this distinction, subtle though real, may give courage to those who hazard their hopes and fortunes with the newer way.

Enslavement encourages fear; coalition creates it. What treatment of a conquered foe promises freedom from fear? Recall Machiavelli's alternates: utterly destroy, or indissolubly integrate. The first is palpably impossible; the second incredibly daring, but it provides us, with some variations, the outline of the third. It may be put thus: enable your former foe to grow strong —materially so that he will be able to carry his own load in the world's march toward economic security;— spiritually so that the energies of his mind and soul shall be directed toward co-operative and creative social and spiritual ends for the world.

Let it be admitted at once that such a proposal is what we have called it—incredibly daring. Even in a day that is seeing new records of heroism written every day all over the earth such daring is beyond us. We may even swing violently to the opposite extreme and say that it is just such a condition that we will fear most. It must not be disposed of, however, by a confession of faintheartedness. Remember: "the only thing we need to fear is fear." The other two methods have proved to be the generators of the fear that has possessed the world; this third method has not been tried. If it is based on an accurate understanding of the human spirit —which, we insist, is substantially the same everywhere despite the differences of cultural veneer that cover it— then we may reasonably expect that it will have a more than fair prospect of success, success at least in terms of reducing if not indeed eliminating the fear of the conquered by the conqueror.

In other words we are confronted by a proposition that will assess enormous psychological costs if we try it. The demand for spiritual hardihood in the form of courage, hope, and confidence will be superlative. Only the dauntless will lead and only the undiscourageable will follow. For it will cost money too, more in the last analysis than either of the other two expedients. It involves exactly what the Vice-President has predicted —the re-education of a new generation of German and Japanese boys and girls. Little wonder the fainthearted sniff contemptuously at the impractical idealism of Mr. Wallace. It is so much easier to keep on thinking of the postwar world in terms of prewar settlements, hoping meantime that *this* time it is going to be different and we can use the old tricks without suffering the old consequences.

[4]

We need, however, to look at this proposition from the other side. All that has been said has arisen out of our concern that we find a method by which we can assure ourselves that nationally we need never again be afraid. But the fear that fathers wars is not our fear alone; *it is also the fear that others may have of us.*

This is a global war; the neurosis of fear is also global. The President is wise in saying that until all fear is banished from every nation everywhere we shall all of us, everywhere, be poisoned by its virus. So long as any are afraid, all are afraid.

For this reason we are under the necessity, from the standpoint of self-interest if no other, to be quite as concerned that others shall not fear *us* as that we shall not fear *them*. The strong man who has no sense of fear is not, by that fact, secure. On the contrary, while he boasts his intrepidity he may be creating a state of mind in another *of which he ought* to be afraid. The boldest man cannot tell what a panicky person will do. And this arises out of the instinctive quality of normal fear. As in infants the fear-response is manifest in the sensation of a loss of support, so in groups the *lack* of some necessary support to life may cause a fear as dangerous as an aggressive threat of violence. This is the psychological factor that gives validity to the claims of the "have not" nations. Economically and politically they may find it hard to make a case; psychologically their case is axiomatic. And this is very important if we are concerned with ridding ourselves of fear—ourselves and them. It is of no use to exhort such people not to be afraid. As well argue with an infant not to gasp when he feels himself falling.

It is precisely this that makes the case for violence so

plausible. The fears that others have felt because of us have pointed out violence to them as the way of escape. Violent conflict produces more fear, however, never less. Even when the conflict is settled and relations are renewed either by subjugation or coalition, the fear still lingers and festers until such a time as it can break forth again into violence. This is true of class war, race war, global war. The reason war, proved to be futile and destructive, is still invoked is that the fear that rationalizes war is an instinct that cannot be eradicated. It can only be educated.

One of the basal factors in social evolution is the possibility of the education of our primitive and undisciplined instincts. We have no hope that fear can be eliminated from the human complex; we should have hopes that it can be educated—fear educated to prudence, prudence vitalized to creative power, as we have put it. In spite of our understanding, we have never done this in the area of political conflicts, although most of our education has been focused on it in our contacts with the material universe and other human beings. Versailles failed because it was based upon policies which deliberately kept fear alive. Fear was regarded as an aid to reconstruction and order, it was not deprecated as a disease and understood as the seed of another war. The sense of frustration the victors imposed on the vanquished was not only humiliating, it was terrifying. Humiliation may sometimes create violence; fear is almost certain to create it. Under the terms of the treaty, it was inevitable that an outbreak should occur.

[5]

We have been contending that the direction in which the fourth freedom leads us is away from the political expedients the past has employed and toward a new goal which, by its deeper understanding of the human spirit, gives promise of success. Manifestly a good deal of educating will have to be done among the timorous whose only reply to the new proposal will be scorn. There are others who will argue that whether the proposal be practical or not, it asks too much of human nature. Perhaps so; but if that is the case, to talk about freedom from fear is pure hypocrisy and the sooner we turn to other matters, the better it will be for our souls.

It is asking too much of politics to do this. There are some scattered diplomatists, who are statesmen as well, who see the problem from this perspective and are talking about it. Premier Jan Smuts in his notable utterance to the House of Commons in October, 1942, said a good deal that had such a focus; and all of his sentiments were summarized in these noble words:

This war is a new crusade, a new fight to the death for man's rights and liberties, and for the personal ideals of man's ethical and spiritual life.

Coming from some publicists that idealism might be nothing more than a lofty cliché. We remember, however, that Smuts was one of the few men who protested immediately and with great vigor after Versailles that grave injustice had been done and that it would be paid for by equally grave consequences. How truly he spoke, so truly indeed that one feels that the words quoted above are not meant to refer exclusively to the rights and liberties, the ideals of man's ethical and spiritual life of the United Nations. The distorted and wicked philosophy of Nazism is a hideous aberration; it is a fantasm born of deep racial fears sharpened and envenomed by the adolescent fears of the son of a drunkard. It knows little or nothing of what we call man's ethical and spiritual life. Smuts, we feel confident from many other wise things he has said, would include all our present adversaries under the aegis of the new crusade. They, no less than we, must be freed from the fears that confuse man's ethical life and debase his spiritual life.

We mention the comment of another who, because she has been all of her life a next door neighbor to Germany, is entitled, more than most to a judgment as to how she is to be dealt with when she is once again brought low. There is much about the recent utterances of Queen Wilhelmina of the Netherlands that is disturbing. She has not, indeed she perhaps cannot, come out of the shell of Dutch imperialism within which her life has been shaped. But whether she has said the last or the wisest word concerning the Dutch colonial empire and the fortunes of three hundred million dark people, she has, in the quotation which follows, responded to an impulse and a conviction that must lie very deep within her. That impulse and wisdom we shall presently point out stems from her Christian heritage. It is appropriate therefore, before we enter a discussion of what the Christian tradition has specifically to say to our problem that the good queen be allowed a word.

The words are quoted by an Associated Press dispatch of November 17, 1942, and are taken from an address she had prepared for delivery at the closing session of the New York *Herald Tribune's* two-day Forum on Current Problems. The report reads:

Queen Wilhelmina of the Netherlands tonight said the United Nations' thirst for revenge after the war would be "great and understandable" but that revenge should not "be our guiding motive."

"Let justice be our aim—justice and firmness tempered by wisdom," she said. "Revenge is barren, except that it breeds revenge," she said. "Impracticable or exorbitant measures are just as bad as no measures at all. That has not always been remembered. Let us not lose sight of it again. We must be firm, realistic, far-sighted. The future of those who come after us is at stake, and for that future we are to a large extent responsible."

Our problem is in the first place a method of dealing with a conquered foe in such a fashion as will contribute to the world-wide effort to eliminate the fears that have plagued our peace. This is principally a political problem as it has been discussed up to this point. Before turning to what is more scrupulously an inquiry into the bearing of the Christian tradition upon the matter, we observe, concerning the Queen's words that the fears which have been spawned of subjugation and coalition are a testimony to them as "impractical . . . exhorbitant measures." Again, no one ever said revenge was the liberator of fear. If we are "firm, realistic, far-sighted" with an eye to "that future for which we are to a large extent responsible," shall we try making our enemy materially strong enough to carry his part of the world's material duties, and spiritually strong enough to turn his mind and soul into creative and co-operative aims? It will take more than firmness, realism, vision. It will take all that plus courage.

Courage is a quality of the spirit. Whence shall our replenishment come?

Part II

"If we go to war, it is from weakness, not from strength. If we arm it is because we are afraid. If we slay our enemies it is because we are too stupid, too cowardly, too slothful to face the strain of making them our friends. If from behind vast armies and navies we hurl defiance at the world, it is because terror has got us by the throat."[1]

We have said that the effort to secure freedom from fear involves first of all a recognition that normal fear is ineradicable from the human composite and for that reason we shall never be quit of it. Our task then is to make use of it, to educate it so that the primitive, untutored instinct may yield its high potential for creative ends. Fear must be taught to become prudence, and prudence must be vitalized into power. This is a spiritual discipline and any treatment of the fourth freedom must allow it priority rating. Our attention, however, has been largely diverted from spiritual disciplines to political expedients. We are afraid of aggressor nations and we propose to overwhelm them primarily, we are told, so that they never again can terrorize the world. This is enormously costly and after it is done the necessity for keeping them harmless will increase the total bill rather than diminish it. We are compelled, in this latter effort, to decide how our conquered foe is to be treated with a view first to abating our fear of him

[1] G. A. Studdert-Kennedy, *The Hardest Part,* New York: Harper & Brothers, 1932.

and finally to freeing ourselves entirely. Three methods have been discussed: keep him in a state of slavery; or keep him strong enough to frighten others we fear and at the same time too weak to threaten us. The former of these two is the ancient imperialistic device that has its practitioners among the fascist dictators and in a few alleged friends of the United Nations; the latter device has rather vigorous and hopeful support on our side from those who still believe in the omnipotence of balance-of-power politics. Whatever else is to be said about them neither of these political designs gives any reason for the hope that fear will diminish under their operation. On the other hand there are circumstances implicit in the nature of these plans that disparage any such hope. It is necessary then—in pursuit of the fourth freedom—to seek a third method. This has been outlined as an effort to help the former enemy to become materially strong enough to bear his full share of the world's physical load, and spiritually strong enough to turn his energies into creative and co-operative effort. It has been argued that this at least looks in the direction of eliminating our fear of him and his fear of us, each of which is as necessary as the other. It involves an outlay of moral and material resourcefulness that appalls by its magnitude, and yet we are exhorted by the President to act in the realization that no cost is too great if it can accomplish this end. In passing it may be pointed out that provision for the material recuperation of our former foe does not involve his rearmament. The process of education involved in the achievement of spiritual strength would, one hopes, point out the unwisdom of militarism and thus reduce the ambition to return to it again.

[1]

The point of view from which these studies have taken direction is the ethical insight of the Judeo-Christian tradition. This has been set over against the political opportunism which is a struggle for power within a social, national or racial group. From the standpoint of political expediency—if freedom from fear is politically expedient—it has been indicated that enslavement and balance-of-power schemes do not stand up under criticism. It remains to ask what can be said for the third expedient from the point of view of the Judeo-Christian tradition. We have thought it politically indefensible. Does it find support in the ethical insights of our religion?

Fear has been the concern of every religion. Voltaire is said to have quipped that religion began when the first knave met the first fool. It is far more likely that if religion had such a low genesis it was when the first knave met the first coward.

Cringing before the riven oak
Mankind the lightning would appease;
In fear the sunset's fire invoke,
Or greet the dawning on his knees.

Whatever else is to be said on the point, it is manifest
that the religious tradition which has nurtured us has
had a good deal to say about fear, its uses and its education. Indeed it is possible to view the Bible as a
dramatic presentation of the conflict between Fear and
Love that was played between the earliest days of the
Hebrew peoples and the end of the first century of
the Christian Era. As if acutely aware of the place
these two titan impulses play in the human struggle
more is said in the Bible about fear than any other elemental urge except love. It is the latter mood that pre-
vails in the New Testament as if in the denouement the
victory were awarded to love. The Bible is not more
than sixty-six verses old before Fear, the villain, enters,
twisting his mustaches and frightening the innocents in
Eden. He is properly disguised as the Deity, but he
works his villainy without giving himself away. "I heard
thy voice in the garden" the man called out, "and
I *was afraid,* because I was naked, and I hid myself."
Nothing of the kind, we retort, and smile to note what
psychologists have told us about the way in which fear
explains itself in terms of the object nearest to it. Something had invaded Eden that was to complicate all life,

something wholly new, for in the last verse of the second chapter, the complete absence of shame—which is mild fear—was sufficiently notable to deserve special comment. That new thing was not an undraped body, it was naked fear.

Fear enters the Biblical drama early, and it leaves only a few moments before the last curtain falls. Forty-four verses from the end we learn of the final foiling of the villain and all those whom he has bewitched. "But the *fearful,* the unbelievers . . . shall have their part in the lake which burneth with fire and brimstone." Furthermore the idyll of Eden that was shattered by the invasion of Fear is restored in the new Jerusalem from which Fear is expelled—a new idyll in which the city's gates "shall not be shut at all by day, for there shall be no night there." An unguarded city, a nightless day— what more perfect symbolism is to be had for a fearless people? The villain Fear is foiled by the hero Love.

The Bible is not only dramatic, it is dogmatic. Love which is the fulfilling of the law is also the conqueror of fear. There is no ambiguity here: "There is no fear in love, for perfect love casteth out fear." The claim is made that it is possible to be free from fear; that the degree of one's freedom from fear is in such proportion as love is dominant; and that perfect freedom from fear is the result of the perfect dominion of love.

This however is a sort of *ex post facto* judgment. The

author of those words speaks far on toward the end of the drama. Is it possible to know how the expectation of ultimate freedom from fear became a part of the dynamics of Judaism? It is important to ask this for the reason that other religions have sought escape from fear by denying its existence. Such efforts are false, says John Macmurray, and false religion says:

Shut your eyes to the things you are afraid of; pretend that everything is for the best in the best of all possible worlds; and there are ways and means of getting the divine powers to your side, so that you will be protected from the things you are afraid of. They may happen to other people but God will see to it that they don't happen to you.[2]

Not that there are no evidences in the Old and New Testaments of a low approach to the problem of fear, blindness in fact; but that in the main the Biblical message is:

Look the facts you are afraid of in the face; see them in all their brutality and ugliness and you will find, not that they are unreal, but that they are not to be feared.[3]

Why are they not to be feared? For three reasons, each of which is abundantly documented by Biblical incident. First: If one stops to look danger in the face he will see that a large proportion of what he sees is illusory, the source of fear is in himself. This will elimi-

[2] *Freedom in the Modern World*, New York: D. Appleton-Century Company, Inc., 1932.
[3] *Op. cit. Freedom in the Modern World*. Vide Supra.

nate some of the trouble. Second: One will also discover that one has considerable resources for overcoming the fear that is real if one will make the effort to use them. Very often, for example, fear of death is a fear of life. Unconfessed sins that make us spiritually unfit to tackle life make us afraid of ourselves, though we mistakenly call it fear of death. The resources of confession are a psychological purge that actually creates a reservoir of courage. Third: it is implicit in our religious faith that after one has exhausted all one's own energies against the assault of fear, God can supply the deficit. Not to escape danger, but to abolish fear. This is what high religion is for, and the martyrs who have gone to their death singing have been its unchallenged witnesses.

This sense of inner resource was a long time developing. For generations God was a capricious ally to the fearful and when He gave strength it was with His strong right arm or by some other external portent of power. In time of danger one fled to the covert of His wings and when the terror was past emerged to sing: "He that dwelleth in the secret place of the most High shall abide under the shadow of the Almighty."

From the sense of God's power surrounding one to the sense of God's presence infusing one is a long pilgrimage, but the latter state produces the greater heroism. When Paul asked: "Who shall separate us from the love of Christ? shall tribulation, or distress, or

persecution, or famine, or nakedness, or peril, or sword?"
—these things that affright us—he had his own answer:
. . . "I am persuaded . . . that height, nor depth, nor
any other creature, shall be able to separate us from the
love of God, which is in Christ Jesus." [4] Such a testimony brings us close to the Bible's final affirmation
about fear in I John 4:18. The Elder John was not
writing about the tempered anxieties that are the fears
of happy and secure folk; he was talking about the fear
that was excruciating—"fear hath torment." It is just
that from which one is to be liberated by love.

There may be some objection to the violence implied
in the description of love's operation on fear. To "cast
out" fear seems more than love is thought able to do.
One conjures up the picture of Love moving adroitly
into the secret chamber of the heart, searching out Hate
and leaping on it, securing it by the scruff of the neck
and tossing it out into the darkness. It is not the sort
of stratagem Love has used in other circumstances. And
yet the word "cast out" is not improperly employed.
Ballo is translated in a variety of ways. It may mean
"to deposit" or "to assault." The primary rendering in
Thayer is: "To throw, either with force or without
force, yet with a purpose, or even carelessly." As light
puts out the dark and as the song assaults the silence,
so love casts out fear.

[4] Rom. 8:35,38.

The year 1942 has brought us many stories of the new heroes of war, but none seems to illustrate better the fact that the sense of God, not as portent but as presence, casts out fear. The three men who were adrift in a rubber raft for thirty-odd days reported how they were free from the fear that all but overwhelmed them when their plane was forced down at sea. They looked the facts of their situation in the face and estimated their chance of rescue. Then they took stock of their resources and divided up the responsibilities of food, navigation and observation. Then they prayed. The story had immense publicity and no doubt touched many a reader with the thorn point of a personal question. How generally was it recognized as a demonstration of the spiritual law: Love casts out fear?

[2]

After all, however, we must allow the skeptics' protest that it was nothing of the sort. Those who have no experience of God cannot accept the story of the derelict seamen as true. To them another approach is to be made. If they prefer, God can be left out of the argument without damaging the principle. It is still demonstrable that love casts out fear even on the lowest human levels.

Common sense supports it and when we deal with our friends its operation is obvious. It can almost be reduced to an equation: more love equals less fear; more fear equals less love. The moment confidence is sullied by suspicion, fear begins to stir; if it is not presently counteracted by a new certainty, fear will cast out love. Manifestly, however, this is an affair between friends, and our problem does not lie in that area since we do not fear our friends. The words: "perfect love casteth out fear" are superfluous among those who love each other except as an admonition to keep one's affections in good working order.

Christian idealism, however, goes ahead and proposes to apply this law to one's enemies and to strangers. This is quite another proposition, but it swings us back into touch again with our suggestion that fear is to be abolished only by treating our fallen enemies after the manner outlined in the third proposal above. The contingency was not unknown to or unanticipated by Jesus. "Ye have heard it said of old time: thou shalt love thy neighbor and hate thine enemy. But I say unto you, Love your enemies and bless them that curse you, do good to them that hate you, and pray for them which despitefully use you." Why, one asks impatiently, should one be so abject? Does not such servility reduce one in the eyes of one's enemy to a level below the despicable? If we feel that way—and we do—it is because spiritually we are still living in the "old time" Jesus was outdating. So far as the treatment of our

enemies is concerned, the last two thousand years might
not have happened.

And yet, Jesus gives the reason for such an attitude.
"That ye may be children of your Father." No senti-
mentality that! No degradation to subhuman levels, but
an elevation to superhuman levels. Not in heaven—by
no means!—but by experiencing a quality of life one
aspect of which we may confidently assert is freedom
from fear. The fact is that the process of educating our
primitive fear instinct has progressed no further than
in the days of Jesus. Perhaps in some eddies on the edge
of the general stream of culture it may have reached a
level beyond prudence and become creative of social
harmony and progress. Unquestionably there have been
heroes in whose spirits the instruction of fear reached
the highest levels of fearlessness. And all of us, at one
time or another have been wistful for it. Yet it cannot
be gainsaid that in the main our treatment of our
enemies, be they erect or prostrate is patterned after the
ancient mandate: "thou shalt love thy neighbor and
hate thine enemy." Twenty centuries are gone and we
are still spiritual midgets.

[3]

This is of course a judgment rendered from the standpoint of the Christian tradition. By no means will all
who stand within that ethical potential feel that its

power should be pointed today in a new direction and in support of a new technique of dealing with enemies. But in any case, we are not free from fear of enemies, and if we are doing more than tossing off a war slogan as we talk about the fourth freedom, we cannot ignore the massive ethical compulsion of love as we seek help in our quest. Our political insights, as we have analyzed them, have not and will not unshackle our timid impulse, nor will they educate our fears beyond the stage of prudence. We do not attempt—more accurately we have not attempted—the method that promises possible success because we are afraid it will not work. The moral insight of the Christian tradition is not accepted because of the current distrust of the effectiveness of a distinctly religious approach to political problems (the perversity against which all we have said is directed). Since this is so, is there any other support available? Is there a convincing word that comes neither from the voice of the political nor the religious prophet? We believe there is; it comes from the psychologist. Not that he is expertly conversant with politics and religion as such; but that the principles which he has discerned as operative in the individual spirit are not dissimilar to those that, in the main, control social behavior.

We talk about United Nations, and the plans for the postwar world, however different in details, are uniform in their quest for the basis for an integrated world. Too long has our international disintegration delayed our coming to full, planetary maturity. Now there is nothing more important to the psychologist than personal integration. It is an old idea, yet it has had its scientific grounds understood only recently. That Jesus talked about it is similar to the fact that Archimedes talked good physics in his day. For in a total view of the universe, all laws, psychical and spiritual, must be congruous. It is more accurate of course to say that in the new physics that recognizes no distinction between physical and spiritual energies, one law governs both manifestations of a central energy.

Physics, of the elementary sort that novices study, says that two objects cannot occupy one space at the same time. Psychology says that two ideas cannot occupy the mind at the same instant. Ethics—not to be overlooked—says that two aims cannot occupy the intention in the same act. To avoid the confusion that attends the efforts of the unwise to subvert these simple propositions, an integration of purpose must be achieved. What this does to physics is no concern of this argument; but psychology agrees with ethics in the metaphorical statement familiar to everybody: "You cannot serve God and Mammon." This is the psychological law of integration, for all it is a verse of Scripture.

Nobody but a moron would spend time trying to put two objects into the same space; and he is a freak of nature who does not have a one-track mind, since no two ideas can ride any one rail. But while we leave it to morons to defy the laws of physics and psychology, we think it the part of wisdom to defy the ethical application of the same law. With complete disregard of moral law we invite a variety of motives to take possession of our spirits.

Not at once, perhaps. We try indecision first, thinking that having *no* single compelling motive is the wisest and easiest way to get along. Or we wait for the pressure or caprice of the moment to determine our intent. This is moral opportunism. It is much like the court provision that commits a child of divorced parents to periods of alternate residence with each. Even though there be genuine fondness between the child and both parents, it is almost certain to develop, sooner or later, that he can no more serve Dad and Mamma, than Dad can serve God and Mammon.

The result of this equivocation is moral confusion and delayed or feeble action. Situations thus encountered generally turn out badly, and before long one is in the grip of moral cynicism. Parallel to moral cynicism is nervous exhaustion—the disintegration of spiritual defeat. John Masefield in a long and searching poem poses the difficulty:

> To pass the wine cup and be witty,
> Water the sands and build the city,

Slaughter like devils and have pity.

. . . . . .

Fashion an altar for a rood,
Defile a continent with blood,
And watch a brother starve for food.[5]

The psychiatrist tries to arrest this when it becomes pathological, and his technique is to seek an interest, manual, mental, or social, around which the frustrated personality can be reintegrated. Psychologically the mooted 1942 Armistice Day speech of General McNair in which he urged his soldiers to have only one aim— to kill and to destroy—is perfectly sound advice whatever one may think of its ethical quality. One thing, however, is disturbing about it: it contributes little to the achievement of the fourth freedom; and, to add another indictment, if it is true, it renders the Christian testimony void and interrupts the proper education of fear by tossing aside the rational restraints the race has built up, and reaches for a gun. Read again the words at the head of this chapter. G. A. Studdert-Kennedy was no sissy; he knew war with terrible intimacy and his diagnosis of the relation between war and violence still stands as unimpeachable.

[4]

We have come to the point in our argument where it is possible to make claim that the ancient Christian

[5] "The Passing Strange," *Poems*, by John Masefield, New York: The Macmillan Company.

prescription for the purgation of fear is politically, morally and psychologically feasible. By the failure of other methods to evict fear and by the practical success of the operation of love, John's venerable word is validated.

The human spirit, we have learned, must be integrated by the gradually growing control of one dominant mood. It would seem plausible to assume that the same necessity is upon the whole of humanity. It is exactly this that the President's exhortation points to if we allow ourselves to see it in its total perspective. But are we yet sure which of our primitive, uninstructed impulses should rule us? We know that fear and rage are more aggressively active today than love is; but is there a reason in the nature of love itself that should constrain our allegiance to it?

We think there is. To alter slightly a famous aphorism: Now abideth fear, rage, and love and the greatest of these is love. We have said repeatedly that fear must be educated to prudence and vitalized to creative power, and that with us the educative process has reached the second stage only. One reason why it is difficult to get past the second stage and into the third is that fear is substantially a protective device; and when it becomes creative, it has lost its essential character. In other words, we are freed from fear by educating it out of its original essence. While it is uniquely fear and performing its protective function, it has little time for anything else. Every impulse is autonomous, authentic, and arbitrary while it lasts. "He does not stop to choose a road who's fleeing for his life." Valuable as the protective function is, it lies on a level of utility far below our creative instincts and demands.

Much the same thing is to be said about rage. To discipline anger requires bringing it under the control of purposes that can be made constructive. Rage itself can build nothing. Hence Motherwell's hope that the enormous power of hate that will be left in Europe when the war is over "may be turned," as he puts it, "against brute nature," in reconstructing the physical life of the Continent.

We conclude then that of these three impulses, love is the greatest because it alone is constructive, it alone can create and sustain growth. But there are three other reasons to support a claim for its superior status. First: love alone can continue as a dominant mood without destroying the spirit. To live in perpetual rage or fear is not only dangerous, it is impossible. The nervous exhaustion each entails can be endured for only the shortest intervals. Perpetual madness is insanity; perpetual fear is psychotic. Second: only love can teach rage and fear how they must behave in decent company. Indeed the whole educative program of the race is carried on through the activity of this good preceptress of the soul. Third: furthermore the fear and rage that are powerful in their elementary stage are progressively weaker, the longer they are sustained. The man in a panic is vulnerable to his adversary in a score of ways: the man in a rage is easy pickings for the assailant who keeps his head. Only love can, by persevering, grow more powerful. Had the race been endowed only with the impulses of anger and fear, humanity would never have survived the shock of the first murder outside Eden.

Love alone is constructive; love alone is tolerable; love alone is teacher; love alone grows strong by growing. It is by man's possession of this strange endowment that his precocity is maintained among his humbler con-geners, and it is by "following after love" that he ascends the long incline toward divinity. Why else have men, by their deepest insights, seen that God is love? Why else is there a turning toward him by all men in myriad ways and for manifold reasons? The Christian doctrine that the universe is the animation of love is more than theology, it is the apotheosis of life. To those who have long been at home with this point of view it is no great surprise to discover a distinguished American scientist writing a book to say that the only hope for the human race lies in educating it in the temper and techniques of love.[6] We love and hate because we are what we are. We must *learn* how to love more and

[6] Karl Menninger, M.D., *Love Against Hate,* New York: Harcourt, Brace and Company, 1942.

hate less. The domain of rage and fear has extended too far and lasted too long. It is necessary that we take the first step that will lead us to a realization that we are afraid because we do not love. It is the necessary second step that commits us to the method of love in seeking to free the world from fear. How timely the Presidential mandate!

[5]

If this is left to politicians, diplomats, and statesmen it will be delayed even beyond the millenniums that separate it from our most hopeful predictions. If, however, it can become a personal discipline with millions of simple-hearted men and women—who are not prejudiced against its political feasibility because it has proved personally impossible for them—things might happen. We do not need to wait until the war is over to release new creative energies into the world. Indeed if when that good day comes there are not already many committed to the way of love, there will be no sudden espousal of the idea at the council tables of the nations. We believe then that those who hold to our great religious tradition must begin work at once, not waiting for the war to stop and the politicians to start.

What to do? Drain off the poison of hate we have allowed to settle in the depressions of our souls. What is hate? Hate is rage compounded with an idea about the cause of fear or anger. Instinctively I recoil from danger or affront. I *think* about you who caused the disturbance and, unless something interferes, my thought determines a course of behavior toward you. I may hate you. Not instinctively, because hate is not instinctive, but rationally, because hate is born of an idea. Since hate is rational, it is subject to rational controls *if they are invoked in time*. If hate smolders, the mind suffocates in its smoke and, without one's knowing it, he rationalizes his hatred in terms of justice. There is a world of difference between the rational control of anger and the rationalizations of hate. This is why those who, for whatever reason, urge the inculcation of hatred as a war necessity, are spreading poison germs among those who fight. It is possible to drain off hate and by so doing to reduce the rigors of our fears.

Not only must we drain it off; we must refuse it tenancy, for it will be back like the fabled seven devils to reoccupy our purged spirits. And perhaps the most effective device for keeping it out of our souls is to make the conscious effort to keep it out of the souls of others. *I can keep others from hating me for the very simple reason that I can keep others from fearing me.* This is a part of the process of exposing fear to education, the only way we are to be rid of it.

But, it is impatiently pointed out, we are not dealing with our friends who sometimes fear us and may, unhappily, hate us; we are dealing with enemies—or will be when the settlement time comes. Is there any preliminary discipline that may be invoked? We think there is. Try to discover in your adversary the things that you are not afraid of. These are the creative powers that he must some day use. This does not mean a shutting of the eyes to the evil—hideous, dark, barbaric, depraved—of which he is both capable and guilty, but opening the eyes to the good in which he is both capable and practiced. There are such elements. Our fighting men recognize them. The courage, devotion, hardihood, ingenuity, skill, ambition of one's foe always elicit the plaudits of a chivalrous adversary. Do we see that these qualities that have been educated for destruction and death are the same qualities that must be educated for construction and life if the world is to endure as the habitation of men? After the war our foe will either be destroyed with his qualities or restored with them. It is the latter that will advance and secure freedom from fear both for ourselves and for him.

And yet this is confessedly most difficult. It even has a taint of disloyalty about it or treason to national aims while we are locked in battle. We will therefore either abandon the effort or turn elsewhere for its practice. Where? If we cannot begin on our enemies, we always have our friends! Can we not make a start with those who are actual or potential allies? It is important to cultivate good will toward those in whom it is not difficult to have confidence. There are those in our neighborhood who need it. What of the segregated in our cities—the negroes, the unassimilated foreigners, the dispossessed? What of Japanese-Americans in their centers of isolation and surveillance?

This is not difficult but neither is it automatic. It calls for the sort of faith in the efficacy of love that is as daring and forthright as the faith others have in enslavement and balances of power. These faiths in units smaller than national states have their advocates and exemplars. Only as others give evidence and practice of their higher confidence will the necessary demonstration of a new international pattern be given.

And it will do more than demonstrate the method by which man ultimately will live if he is not miserably to die. It will increase our own confidence in the efficacy of love; it will develop spiritual skill and power by the regular flexing of our spiritual muscles; and it will add to that aggregate of good will among the sons of men which, when it reaches the full level of our personal, social and national life, will overflood the world.

If we don't? Every time I fear, or hate, or scorn, I push the possibility of man's freedom from fear one step further beyond the reach of the world. It has been simply put in a quatrain. Its wisdom and its tenderness are a benediction, and its words linger hauntingly.

When I am dead what I have felt so long
My soul shall know in clearer purer light;
That where I loathed and hated I was wrong;
That where I loved and pitied I was right.[7]

That seems to be the right way to win freedom from fear now. We must not wait 'til we are dead.

[7] "Illumination," taken from *Songs and Laughter*, by Arthur Guiterman, published and copyright by E. P. Dutton & Co., Inc., New York.

In the beginning, God . . .
Genesis 1:1

The grace of our Lord Jesus Christ be with you all. Amen.
Rev. 22:21

Live among men as if God beheld you;
Speak to God as if men were listening.
SENECA: Epistles

A mighty fortress is our God
A bulwark never failing;
Our helper amid the flood
Of mortal ills prevailing.
MARTIN LUTHER

Our father's God, to thee,
Author of liberty,
To Thee we sing.
S. F. SMITH

Conclusion
—AND GOD

"I am not suggesting that the world has no need of sound economy, or of automatic machinery. And I am not suggesting that professional economists give up their dreary science and begin plugging for philosophy, ethics and religion. I am merely denying that the sick soul of the world can be made well by straightening out its financial affairs." [1]

Briefly to recapitulate. The effort made in these pages has not been to diagnose the sickness of the soul of the

[1] Ted Robinson, the Philosopher of Folly. Cleveland *Plain Dealer.*

world, but to examine the cure that the President has prescribed in the Four Freedoms. That it is a sickness of the soul has made it necessary to seek for spiritual medicaments. Freedom is the state of spiritual health; lack of freedom is pernicious spiritual anemia. Such nostrums as the politicians compound may promise to palliate or anesthetize the pain, but he is a charlatan who guarantees a cure with political pills. The unguents that will soothe a rash cannot silence a heart murmur.

We have sought to understand freedom of speech, freedom of religion, freedom from want and freedom from fear as four of the goals to be won in the total liberation of the human spirit; and anxiety has been frequently expressed lest the use of this quartet of great ideals should fall to the level of slogan shouting, with the subsequent demand of the people, after the military war is over, that politicians and statesmen make good on their promises. The sorry end of that would be the popular cynicism about freedom which will be an invitation to the fascist to come in with his political quackery that soothes humanity only in order that it may shackle man's spirit. Thus freedom of speech is a spiritual endowment that is implicit in the moral quality of human communication by language; freedom of a man's right to establish contact with the object of his ultimate devotion is a spiritual franchise which can be abridged only by a man himself. Freedom from want involves adequate food, shelter, clothes, work, medical

care and a few other essentials, but if one's spiritual
resources by which all judgments of surplus and deficit,
appetite and repugnance are formed, the satisfactions
of physical desires may become the cause of new conflicts and of further denials of freedom. Freedom from
fear is more obviously a matter of spirit than any of the
other three and is basal to their exercise. Through the
very nature of fear, however, we cannot get rid of it,
nor do we wish to be. In order that it may be used in the
creative ways for which it seems to have been designed
it must be educated. As native panic, it is dangerous
and weak, as prudence, it is safe and conservative.
When prudence is spiritually motivated and vitalized it
grows from mere caution to the full stature of creativity.
It is the spiritually creative alone who are the spiritually
free. Love is the energy of creation.

This has had the result, in the author's mind at least,
of converting the President's war aims for the whole
world into a spiritual crusade. To those who share the
Judeo-Christian religious heritage, such an enterprise
should be neither strange nor daunting. In those periods
of its greatest power and through the insights of its
greatest prophets, our religion has never been committed
to anything else. If then the President has rephrased an
it in its proper perspectives—historic and spiritual—
ancient commission, and if those who accept it can keep
we have a task and a goal worthy of all our blood, sweat,

toil, and tears; and one may add—worthy of our budgets and our prayers.

[1]

There is, therefore, a certain fitness in bringing such a discussion to a close by relating it to the Central Reality. Some, of course, will wonder why God must be lugged in at the end of every argument, either by prayer or expletive. Except to say that such a comment is a symptom of the world's sickness—the egoism that has reached its most loathsome form in the soul of Germany, and that is latent in every soul—we pass on to other matters, for the relevance of God to everything requires a discussion as vast as the idea itself. The fact is, from the standpoint of our religious tradition, God *is* the center of spiritual gravity by which we judge and maintain all spiritual equilibrium. Such times as our own seem to provide a sort of tolerance for the idea of God, and it is sure to be exploited by all manner of men. The point of our use, both of the current deference to God and of the idea itself, is that we shall not win the Four Freedoms without winning God. He is not an addendum to the President's statement of war aims. Indeed we cannot speak of God as a war aim or an embellishment on accepted goals. We must, however, be confronted by the fact that the spiritual quest upon which we have embarked will not be successful except it ends in a new apprehension of the Divine. Let it be put even more abruptly: the Four Freedoms, aims though they be, can never be ends in themselves lest, paradoxically enough, they become the instruments of further enslavement. They can only be means to an eternal end—the freedom of the human soul by its enslavement to God. This is not double talk. St. Paul made familiar use of it in his standard discussions of spiritual freedom. He who was "delivered from the bondage of corruption" was to pass "into the glorious liberty of the children of God" (Rom. 8:21) by being a prisoner of Jesus Christ. The paradox is loftily expressed in a variety of ways in the vast literature of religious devotion.

[2]

It is possible to sharpen our focus by pointing out what Santayana has called "the only two radical alternatives."

There are only two radical alternatives open to human faith. Both are hypotheses. To accept either is to run a risk, to lay a wager; but the gamble is laid upon us by life itself. You may choose the broad and obvious path of heathen philosophy, fancifully decorated with some heathen religion. . . . But there is an alternative, which is to believe in the human heart, to believe in the supernatural, to refuse to follow the great heathen procession except perfunctorily or provisionally. . . . We impose on all natural facts and on all natural desires a supernatural interpretation. . . . I admit that heathen philosophers may judge a supernatural reinstatement of the human heart to be a pathetic fallacy, yet the believer in a divine heart is not without many a confirmation of his faith by his own experience and by the fruits which this faith has always borne among the faithful.[2]

We may not altogether like the words Caleb Weatherbee uses, but we shall not mistake his meaning if for "the human heart" and "the supernatural" we substitute "the human spirit" and "God." If there are fallacies beneath such faith we shall allow time elsewhere for the philosophers to point them out. Our task is simpler and less indirect. We of the Western world have accepted the "gamble that is laid upon us by life itself." There has been something about the hilarity with which we have placed our bets that is heart warming. No niggardly gamblers we. For the most part also we have been sporting in accepting our losses, for our bets have not paid off. Now we are betting stakes so measurelessly high that we are almost afraid of our daring. But what is the commitment of life, military and civilian, to the winning of a war for the freedom of everybody, but a colossal wager on Freedom to win, place or show? We must gamble wisely—if gamble we must. It will help us then, to see why we guessed wrong before?

[2] George Santayana, *The Last Puritan*, New York: Charles Scribner's Sons, 1936, pp 189-190.

[3]

Hocking of Harvard has given new meaning to the
old phrase "a lost world." Not doomed or damned, but
bewildered. It is only a slightly different use of the word
when it describes the gambler's ill fortune. The world is
lost; we have lost the world. Let us examine the bewilderment that has vitiated our culture.

We have lost our sense of direction. During the
recent decades we have been all dressed up but we have
been quarreling about our destination. It surely was not
the war we headed into. Where then were we going?
We simply didn't know. The notion that progress was
automatic and that we would go forward toward two
full dinner pails anyway, was still fondly believed during the twenties. The goal of a classless society, initiated
by violence and sustained by socialism was before the
eager, hollow eyes of the Russians and was winning
acceptance all over the world. We had said the word
"democracy" so often that we almost believed it to be
a sort of magic that could change the world by waving
a ballot. We had a series of beautiful buildings in
Geneva that housed a dream of world unification within
a league and thought that having erected a home for a
league, we had a bona fide tenant. It is true to say,
appalling though it is, that for the past twenty-five years
or more none could speak truly and point out any one

unanimously accepted direction for individual and national life. It was as if—to return to Santayana's gambler—we were betting on horses all running in different directions toward different finish lines.

Added to this conflict about directions has been the dispute about the meaning of our quest. Some have followed the lead of others without asking where they were going or what they were going for. To those who insisted on knowing what it was all about, the most persuasive answers were given by a certain school of psychologists who said the question was irrelevant since we go where our impulses lead us. And if inquiry sought where that is, another group replied that it was foolish to ask oneself such a question, since any answer would be a rationalization of subconscious yearnings or impulses and would therefore be wrong! Education, democratic and dispassionate, was the accomplice and evangelist of this jaunty nihilism, and the higher levels of our culture were so tainted by it that music, art, and literature appeared in some respects heedless of our drifting or disinclined to understand or arrest it. On the lower levels, business and politics found it a condition to be exploited, sometimes for good, often for evil.

It was not alone lost direction and lost meaning that left us befuddled. We lost our nerve. Where the issues of destiny were clear and their directions unmistakable, we had little strength of spirit to act. Life was enervated

by indecision and doubt; life that is sheer, naked, elemental and indestructible power went flaccid, infirm,
languid. It took the shock of a massive, barbaric terror
to straighten us up morally, to make us realize the
measure of our spiritual feebleness, and to ask for new
direction, new meaning, new power.

We had gambled unwisely or had sought to escape
the "risk . . . the wager . . . the gamble . . . laid
upon us by life itself." In the meantime a fantastically
swollen egotist set about to give order to the world. He
chose a direction to which all the world was to conform;
he chose meanings of life that all men were to be compelled to accept, and he offered life, nerve, "strength
through joy," to a nation whose bewilderment had perhaps been the most bitter and most dark. But *Mein
Kampf* has not proved to be the answer, and the Four
Horses that today race across Europe are not the nags
to bet on.

[4]

Lost direction, lost meaning, lost strength; our gamble
was not conspicuously successful. Immediately there
returns to sight a first century Figure, and to mind there
returns something he once said to his generation. "I am
the way (direction), the truth (meaning), the life
(strength)." One also remembers that for twenty centuries he has been urging those who feel the risk that

life lays upon them, to choose his way, and those who have dared have been the winners. This is not luck. There is something in the nature of things that fits the direction he took, that supports the meanings he gave to life, and that co-operates with the energies he releases into life. We are now in the process of preparing ourselves and the whole world for a new adventure in living. The changes that are to come will introduce novelty into national group, social, cultural and economic relations. Some will resist; they will say that what we need is not a new direction, a new understanding, a new energy. On the contrary they will urge that we try the old ways again in the hope that this time they will not betray us. These gamblers will back the same old plugs with a pathetic and maudlin hope that they have one last winning race left in their spavined, wind-broken carcasses. The struggle between those who want a return to the old ways and those who will feel the adventurous hope of the new is soon to be joined. We cannot be too well prepared to meet its shock and to combat its strategy.

If we are to have another chance we must be sure which area of the struggle our strength will serve best. There are two aspects to every problem—the mechanical and the moral. The former deals with the way the matter is to be handled, the latter will determine the spirit by which the process is guided. Unless we understand for which of these our aptitudes and skills have fitted us, we can easily make a nuisance of ourselves. For this reason the technical problems involved in bringing the new world to order must be left to skilled and practiced hands. Good will alone will not set new boundaries in Europe, nor will the most elevated moral idealism alone stop the ravages of pestilence and hunger.

At the same time we must not allow it to be forgotten that the making of the new world is doomed to confusion if it is not undergirded by certain moral judgments which no expediency of the moment can safely set aside. Questions of human rights and obligations, questions of rigor and conciliation—these will yield to no comptometer; they must be settled by a spiritual sensitiveness kept acute by the highest interests of God and man. An understanding of this will prevent the Christian fellowship from speaking where it has no competence; it will also forbid its silence where it ought to speak. Was not the supreme tragedy of the League's failure the fact that so perfect a mechanism should have lacked the perfect spirit? It became a machine, that, wanting the proper spirit to guide it, was despoiled by a malevolent spirit that had hated it from the beginning.

[5]

In the most sententious and in some respects the most significant of the parables of Jesus there is an idea that is fruitful in the present context. There are only fifteen words in the reference: "the slave abideth not in the house forever, but the son abideth ever," [3] and it occurs in connection with the more famous aphorism about the relation of the knowledge of truth to the experience of freedom (John 35:32). The point is clear: Freedom is the sensation of feeling at home. Because this is important to a concluding comment, a brief extension of the principle is pertinent.

Freedom is feeling at home. To be socially free—at ease, if you will—involves being at home with the amenities of society. Mrs. Emily Post is supposed to be the liberator of those who are unhappy slaves to maladroitness and embarrassment. To be mechanically free in a shop means to be at home with belt, wheel, and tool; to be intellectually free means to move among ideas without awkwardness or confusion. To be politically free within a given group means to be at home in society; to be spiritually free means to be at home in the universe.

No clearer contrast can be drawn than that between the slave in the house and the son. They inhabit the same space, use the same things, speak the same language, and in most respects, live the same life. The difference in status, however, is definitive—one is at

[3] John 8:35.

home and will be there forever; the other is not at home at all and will not be there long, he hopes.

The whole problem of the establishment of freedom in the world is, therefore, the problem first of creating a home out of the present chaos, and second to so organize and maintain the world that all will feel at home in it. That this has never been the case hitherto is notorious. The status of physical, social, political and spiritual slavery has been the miserable lot of most of the sons of men. To set them free, to confer the status of sonship—or to allow them full liberty to win it— is the mandate that this desperate hour commits to us. The day of freedom—be it segmented into four or forty parts—is waiting to dawn, and the hope of the nations as never before is that all men shall be free in the house, no longer awkward, or unhappy, or ashamed. With a realization for the first time in history that all men *can* be free, the quest for freedom will not await concessions from the lords of earth. Today an old status has become a new sin—the sin of consenting to bondage; and the mood of expiation is abroad in the world as never before.

In his broadcast of December 28 Vice-President Wallace pledged his faith to two world ideals, "liberty and unity." Such unity as the world has known in the past has been either fortuitous or political. It is proposed now that the unity to come will be planned on the basis of certain moral concepts about man and secured by appropriate political techniques. Fundamental in any understanding of unity is consent to the experience of liberty out of which unity comes. The unity that is factitious lacks the proper spirit to safeguard it; the unity that is forced is mass servility. Tyrants before now have been allies; unity comes only to those who know and trust the right to be free.

For this reason the meaning and realization of freedom for all must be agreed upon before unity with all can be undertaken. So long as there are those within a social or political group who believe in freedom for themselves or their class alone, social and political cohesion is a fraud. So long as there are nations in the world who believe in liberty only for themselves and their fellow nationals, the idea of world unity is chimerical. To talk about it deceives none but those who have been encysted within the pride of race or class, a condition which is as hopeless as it is ancient. We can talk and plan for a united world only after we have conceded the right to freedom to everybody everywhere—freedom of speech and religion; freedom from want and fear.

[6]

We return then to the proposition with which we started. The proud boast of the captain who held Paul prisoner, that he had paid for his political freedom with big money, reflects the ancient and mistaken idea that freedom can be bought and sold, conferred or withdrawn. Paul's confident reply that his freedom was his birthright showed an understanding that rested on much higher presuppositions. But beyond and above the experience of free citizenship as an accident of birth is the concept of freedom as an endowment of every human soul—as the essence indeed of the spirit. It is this third great idea that nurtured the feeble infant of 1776, now grown to such a giant. And the inspiration of that cardinal tenet of our democratic faith came from the deep spiritual reservoir of our hoary religious heritage. To forget this is to invite confusion again; to deny it is to repudiate our faith, to treat it casually or as a thing to pawn is to cast away our spiritual estate. It is to the preservation and extension of nothing less than this that the President has committed America.

The final word has to do with the ultimate matter. No one with orderly senses will think or say that it is easy to keep before one the spiritual aspects and aims of the present turmoil. War is such a mundane and monopolistic affair; it wants all our things, our time, and our intentions. And while from out of the terror and the din of battle come those occasional tender and moving stories about men who have prayed in the foxholes of Bataan and on rafts adrift beneath the insufferable sun, for most of the time the intimations of the spirit are muted or dumb. Yet it is important to keep oneself sensitive to them. Pasteur's final counsel to his students was: "Young men, have confidence in those powerful and safe methods, of which we do not yet know all the secrets. And whatever your career may be, do not let yourselves become tainted by a deprecating and barren skepticism; do not let yourselves be discouraged by the sadness of certain hours that pass over nations." We must be willing even to go beyond such a mood of caution to a more aggressive quality of faith— faith that is essentially moral in its unwillingness to delay action until perfect certainty is won. This is the sort of thing Raymond Moley wrote about in his *Newsweek* editorial of December 28, 1942. "Eighteenth century Democrats," he said, "were wrong in their claim that perfection could come through cold reason alone . . . . The religious idea of perfectibility kept civilization alive through centuries of darkness. It taught the pursuit of perfection in spite of endless failure. 'Be ye therefore perfect as your Heavenly Father is perfect.'"

Even if such intimations should come regularly— these stories of prayer and confidence, or should create a new genre in the reports of war correspondents, or become as routine and copious as casualty lists, the mystery of the experience would remain unsolved. So wise a man as Santayana never got beyond the rim of that enigma. "I admit that heathen philosophers may judge a supernatural reinstatement of the human heart to be a pathetic fallacy, yet the believer in a divine heart is not without many a confirmation of his faith." There may be cabalists who know the secret, as there are cynics who scorn it, but the believer is not without many a confirmation of his faith. The fact of mystery, the realization of the spirit, the "reinstatement of the human heart"—these have won a new tolerance since the great debacle moved toward us. It may be that we are afraid, and mistake our fear for faith. One cannot say, but it might be interesting, revolutionary even, if our attempt to win freedom for the human spirit all over the world became the opening skirmish of a struggle that ultimately left us all free, unafraid, credulous, and wondering.

There is a parable of freedom in an old record. It tells how one who was in prison and chained to guards, won strange liberty. Let the story bear its own witness. Other comment is forborne.

And when he (Herod) had apprehended him (Peter), he put him in prison, and delivered him to four quaternions of soldiers to keep him. . . . Peter therefore was kept in prison; but prayer was made without ceasing of the church unto God for him.

And when Herod would have brought him forth, the same night Peter was sleeping between two soldiers, bound with two chains: and the keepers before the door kept the prison.

And behold, the angel of the Lord came upon him and a light shined in the prison: and he smote Peter on the side, and raised him up saying: Arise up quickly. And his chains fell off from his hands.

And the angel said unto him, Gird thyself, and bind on thy sandals. And so he did. And he saith unto him, Cast thy garment about thee, and follow me.

And he went out, and followed him; and wist not that it was true which was done by the angel; but thought he saw a vision.

ACTS 12:4-9

THE END